FINDING EARTH, FINDING SOUL

FINDING EARTH, FINDING SOUL

The invisible path to authentic leadership

Tim Macartney

Mona BOOKS

First published in 2007 by
Mona Press, Embercombe,
Higher Ashton, Devon, EX6 7QT, England

Re-printed with a foreword by the author and minor amendments in 2013.

Distributed by
UIT / Green Books
PO Box 145, Cambridge, CB4 1GQ, England
+44 1223 302 041   www.greenbooks.co.uk

Photograph of River Li at Xing Ping on pages 168-9 © Gerald Gay

Typeset by Kevin Mount, DeMo

Printed by Page Bros. (Norwich) Ltd.

ISBN 978 1 903998 99 1

10 9 8 7 6 5 4 3

for the invisible path
that, true to its nature,
guides us unseen

CONTENTS

Nearly six years have passed since *Finding Earth, Finding Soul* was first published. In that time some moments of significance have occurred.

From their home in the Sierra Madre mountains of Colombia, the Kogi people have alerted the 'younger brother' to the consequences of his ignorant assault on our Earth, through Alan Ereira's film *Aluna* (launched November 2013); the ash trees of Europe are dying in their millions; and the suffering of countless people in Syria, Egypt, Palestine and Iraq, to name just a few, burns its harsh truth into our eyes and ears each day. At the same time, wolves run wild again in places around the world where a few years ago only their half-remembered shadow remained; a Maasai village in Kenya has new hope because a Devon farmer had the courage to allow a personal tragedy to spur an act of profound generosity; a lawyer friend continues her courageous and loving journey to bring about a law against ecocide; a small girl shares a treasured possession with a friend; and my potatoes are safely stored.

As I write, first light threads into the disappearing night, and colour, scent and sound announce a new day. I wonder, as I have wondered so many times before, what it is that will awaken us to the unfolding tragedy of a deeply compromised future. I am now convinced that we cannot step past what has been set in motion. We have gone too far and for too long. We will be confronted by the consequences. Nevertheless, we can mitigate these consequences, learn from our mistakes, and, walking more gracefully, realise the world of our longing. We can make sense of our past by committing to the future and taking action now.

A short distance up the hill behind my house, a man of great heart and determination will soon gather his men and place brick upon brick to breathe new hope into lives almost broken by drugs, alcohol and a punitive system which sets retribution ahead of rehabilitation. We can do the same. These three questions may help:

* What is it that I most deeply and profoundly love?
* What are my deepest and most profound gifts?
* What are my deepest and most profound responsibilities?

Ask the questions, align the answers, and then using the answers as a navigational tool, commit to action.

The 'younger brother' can learn and change.
The 'younger brother' can meet the challenge of his rite of passage and grow up.
The world of our longing is within reach, but first we have to get out of the chair, link hands, take a step, and learn to walk anew.

Tim Macartney
Embercombe
October 2013

ACKNOWLEDGEMENTS

There are many who have assisted me in the writing of this book in some way. Those that have been prominent are listed here:

Azul-Valerié Thomé – first and foremost, without whose support, encouragement, insistence, cajoling and challenge, I might never have written even the first word; **Jonathan Snell** – for a walk in Haldon Forest that brought me to the foot of the mountain; **David Williams** – my editor, for so sensitively helping me to sort the wheat from the chaff; **Elizabeth Gorla** – for always being there, and telling me how it is; **Lindsay Levin** – for feedback that at the same time was encouraging, critical, and insightful; **Rocky**, **Pearl**, **Sig** and **Willow** – for steadfast friendship, encouragement and support in the early days when self-doubt threatened my resolve; **Monty Don** – for an article in a Sunday paper that has never left me; **Henry Williamson** – for inspiring me, sowing a seed, getting it wrong, and never giving up; **The Wolf** – for so much inspiration, information, and challenge: even the betrayal that spurred my absolute determination to walk away and more courageously lead my own life; **The Erraid Community** – for a safe haven and the privilege of sharing their isle; the many children and young people I know and love, in whose eyes I saw the necessity of finding words that might touch hearts; the gardens I have gardened – for impeccable spiritual teaching; the ravens, the cow and calves, the sea otters, the sea birds, the sheep, the seals, the mouse, the tiny and the huge – for lessons in how to be human; the clouds, the sun, the day and the night, the sea, the streams, the rain, the shadows, the moon, the flowers, the trees, the rocks, the earth, Pier Cottage, Gleann an Teampull, Cnoc Mor, the seen and the unseen – for lessons in seeing beyond.

This book is about journey – getting lost and finding a way. It is also about waking up to life. It is about self-responsibility, inspiration, and leadership. It is, in effect, about healing.

If, in whatever capacity we exert influence, we as a people were to stand up now, and having searched in our hearts for courage, choose to make a stand and say 'No more'.

If we were to accept our own culpability, yet not be shamed by it, rather allowing it to fuel our determination, and become involved in the shaping of our future.

If we were to put aside the saddening weariness of standing on the sidelines and understand that the earth calls us to action.

If we could understand that we are all aunts and uncles, sisters and brothers, mothers and fathers, to each other – that the children are all our children.

If we were to accept the fact that no-one is going to lead us away from the gathering storm but that we have to, all of us, each single one, become the leader and walk towards the storm, trusting that others will follow.

If we can bring everything that is most beautiful and most powerful in ourselves and offer this as our contribution.

If, with the exigencies of our work, we could yet assert that nothing is worth the betrayal of our dreams, our spiritual necessity to find meaning, learn and grow.

If we can do this – and we can if we choose – then this period of human history will be the time that humanity chooses to honour the gift of life and come of age, and it will be a time of great celebration.

There are things worth fighting for, and one of them is the knowledge that in the time that we had, we tasted life as fully as our talents, our imagination, and our circumstances allowed. To know that we played it safe, wasted it, threw it away, or compromised our deeper intention, is to invite grief. There is nothing boring about life, and there is no such thing as a boring person who is walking their life with courage and energy. Boredom is reserved for those of us who are failing ourselves by not applying whatever energy or resolve is needed to locate our path and then step onto it.

My hope is that this book will be read by business leaders and environmental activists, by mothers working at home and members of parliament, by the unemployed and the over-employed, by the elderly and the forever young. For we are one people and we have to find ourselves again in order that we might find each other.

> Treat the Earth well. It was not given to you by your parents,
> it was loaned to you by your children. We do not inherit the
> Earth from our ancestors, we borrow it from our children.
> – Native American proverb

I have a foot in two worlds. There have been times when these two worlds have been at war with each other. One part of me turns always to the mystery of living, pauses in mid-breath, and stares awed, shocked at the beauty of earth, water, air and fire. Another part loves the business of business, winning through, communicating, making deals, striving to deliver results, and celebrating them. Of course, intrinsically the two worlds do not have to be in conflict, but in my case they were. Looking back, I cannot see how it might have been otherwise. I am capable of being immensely stubborn, even in the face of overwhelming evidence suggesting that a change in course might serve me and others well. Because of this I have sometimes found myself penned in a cage of my own making and incurring rather more pain, discomfort, and distress than the situation called for. The notion of making a mistake once and then never repeating the error is incomprehensible to me. On most occasions I have preferred to resemble the motion of a fence post rammer. This is a large and heavy tool that is shaped like a drainpipe, closed at one end, and with two handles on either side. The fence post is set in position and the rammer placed like a sleeve over the top. You can then pound the stake by repeatedly lifting the rammer and heaving downwards. Very satisfying for the rammer, less so for the stake, especially if as a tree you dreamed of being the mast on a ship, or a nicely turned doorknob. The two worlds stand together like neighbours conversing over the garden fence, posturing, dropping names, uneasy and yet hopeful of friendship. When I look back I see how the dilemma described by these two worlds – the meaning of the symbols that each represents within me – has reverberated throughout my childhood and adult life. Only recently has it fully made sense, and even so it is a layered enquiry that leads me deeper as I dare to question more.

I am the man who, when away from the enchantment of the night sky, the scent of the orchard in late spring, away from the land he loves, walking through the portals of some corporate giant, feels a kind of tearing, a dislocation, a vague panic that I might not find my way back.

I am in love with trees, with sunlight splashed on dew-soaked grass, with the wind that lifts my thoughts and shows me the horizon; with the quiet earth from whose mystery comes the whispered memories of lives past and those still dreaming themselves awake. Yet, over the past eighteen years, I have found myself drawn to conversation with business and specifically the women and men who inhabit business as leaders and managers.

In the late 1970s and early 1980s I had worn many different cloaks, experimenting, tasting life, getting bruised, picking myself up, walking on. I couldn't have cared less about careers or money. I just wanted freedom and the knowledge that I was walking with destiny towards some kind of deeper presence with life. The trouble was that, imbued with a fertile and hyperactive imagination, I could usually fool myself into believing anything. In this way I successfully interpreted many bizarre misadventures as the dalliances afforded by the truly inspired. I had intimations of what my life could be, but I couldn't find the way, and I couldn't find the will. Exhausted with a hedonistic lifestyle that demanded immense reservoirs of energy and time, a belief in the future that sapped the lifeblood out of any current endeavour, and a well-practised capacity for avoiding uncomfortable truths, I had beached myself on a rocky shore of my own making. I found myself confronted with the fact that, while I had many dreams, plans, and ambitions, I hadn't really achieved anything of which I could be proud. All I knew was that I needed a rest and some rehabilitation. Working as a trainee gardener at Plas Newydd, a National Trust estate, gave me time to think. It also reminded me of how much I loved and appreciated working outdoors with trees, shrubs and flowers. When the training came to an end I took up a position as gardener at a management training centre in North Wales, Limestone Manor.

I walked into the walled garden at Limestone Manor and knew in some sense that I had found a place where I could nurture a garden that could speak to others. It was a stage waiting. That this place drew large numbers of business executives for leadership, team and personal development, seemed perfect. I was angry with the devastation that big business so casually wreaked upon our environment, and upon fragile communities both at home and abroad. I was dismayed with what I saw as the developed world's collective gullibility in swallowing wholesale the pervasive marketing myth of happiness sustained by ongoing, endless, endemic, massive over-consumption, and the disregard that accompanied it for those excluded from membership.

My anger was strongly permeated with sadness, idealism, and a desire to communicate. In contemplating battle with the enemy, the image of a fifth-columnist gardener, somehow quietly undermining the focused resolve of Britain's business best, was deeply appealing even if how this was to be achieved remained comfortingly vague, and the goal itself intellectually vapid.

Time passed and I was shocked to find that the business executives I met were often more generous, more open, more interesting than the subculture with which I had chosen to identify myself. Eventually the temptation became too strong. I went over the wall, changed costume, and began doing something different. I never left the garden; it remained in my heart. A talisman. A tableau occasionally illuminated by the flickering light of remembered intention. Going over the wall eventually took me to London, first as a visitor, and then to live. The garden became a memory and I almost grew accustomed to my suit. Although the candle flame guttered and shrunk it never actually went out. The garden that continued to live within me was not the dream of returning to my former life, but the fierce desire to find a way in which I could bring my whole self, my true authentic self, into the centre of my life. In my work and in all my relationships I have been striving for this ever since.

We all search for fulfilment from work in one way or another, and all learn of this sooner or later, either through the joy of discovery or the disappointment of lost opportunities. Disappointment need not dominate the horizon, but if this is to be avoided we have to turn and face our fears. The dreams and fantasies of our youth reveal much that can and should inform our adult journey. No measure of security is worth losing sight of the joy that comes from living the adventure that once possessed your heart and sent you sleepless into the night. We are born to journey, to explore and discover, to renew ourselves in the gardens of our choosing. Outside of this lies loneliness and a separation from ourselves, from others, from flowers, from life.

Life presents us with challenges, and we strengthen ourselves, learn and grow, by meeting these challenges and finding our way. This is a spiritual path. There are many who once dwelt in their own garden and who, like me, set off into adulthood and found themselves losing everything that they had once thought of as precious and valuable. What do you do as a young man or woman when you discover that you have ideals and you want to contribute, and that the prevailing attitudes of society, while seeming to endorse these sentiments, actually despise them? We have those who attempt to choose work that encompasses some measure of vocation, and for them we reserve our greatest contempt. Teachers go on and on attempting to clear up the mess that parents, government, and our collective society have spread so generously before them. Nurses are engaged in an endless struggle with indifference. Social workers confront an ocean of unhappiness, knowing that any talk of compassion will not extend to them but will be cynically reserved for those on whom we have already turned our backs, who exist in some far away land on the other side of town. This way we never have to confront what is ours. We are contemptuous of our politicians, yet they look remarkably like you or me. Perhaps they represent us more truly than we ever imagined. I am sure that many enter politics inspired by a desire to make a difference, to contribute to society and give of their best. Yet somehow, listening to them, watching the machinations of the party whips in Britain's celebrated political system, I wonder how long most ideals survive the demand to conform and get in line.

There are many kinds of garden and not all of them grow flowers and vegetables, but all are places of joy, all celebrate the human spirit, all speak of freedom, and all feed and nourish us – old and young. This book is for those who want to fan their candle flame a little brighter, to feel its heat as it uncoils and stretches, luxuriating. I think that our organisations need to remember the garden and revere the spirit that it engenders. I think they need to understand that humans cannot live with themselves when the gap between what brings meaning and purpose and the routine of daily work becomes a gulf, a void of indifference, a bleak vacuum that claims not only the present but the future. I think that we need to bring the orchard into our daily lives and plant things of beauty in every nook and cranny. For most it is not a question of leaving to do something different. It is more challenging than that, and it certainly requires more imagination and determination. It is about remembering who we are and having the courage to fight for the life we yearn for. It is a beautiful battle, a battle fit for heroes and sheroes. It is a question of spirit and of demanding the right to live lives that have meaning. It is a quest and a way of seeking. It is a journey. We have to reclaim the garden.

There are many kinds of dreams and all of them are important. The dreams we have in sleep have always fascinated human beings and are subject to many studies, whilst remaining enigmatic, mysterious, and shadowed, as if existing the other side of the river Styx. Occasionally we will experience a dream that seems to speak louder than all the rest. Sometimes a dream will present itself so emphatically that it is as if the universe itself has spoken to us. I had one such dream. This dream opened a door, and showed me what lay beyond and behind me. It is from this dream that the metaphor of 'the invisible path' emerged. Incorporated within this dream is the notion of 'journey'. Journeys are rarely linear. They wind between the past, present, and future, they are unpredictable, and they confront us with ourselves. Journeys in thought, in feeling, in imagination, or in physical activity, all tend towards the creation of a weave or braid. You and I, we are so much of everything, woven into a single being. Or so it seems. The narrative of this book works in the same way. It braids a journey of self-discovery with the quest for meaningful work, with different gardens of endeavour, with the small and the big, the ugly and the beautiful. It seeks to articulate and illuminate some of the hardship and joy in which we as men and women in the 'developed' world find ourselves embroiled. Allow yourself to be cloaked in what is sometimes invisible. Allow yourself to experience without demanding immediate understanding. Sooner or later you will gain height and see the terrain of your journey with perspective. I love to walk in open country without a map. This way I name my own mountains, and allow my adventures their privilege of surprise.

CHAPTER ONE

The dream pathway, the island, and the garden

THE DREAM PATHWAY

Unseen by me, San Francisco became bathed in golden light, illuminated in colour, warmth, and the promise of renewal. I lay asleep in my bed at the Palace Hotel, and I was dreaming. The night before I had stood by my hotel window looking out across the city, the air conditioning switched off and sharing the quietness with the stars that I knew from my home in Devon, England. I spoke into the night, asking to see the doorway, the gate through which I could touch the people I would meet the following day. I felt good. I had been in similar situations many times – nothing planned, random strands of thought that jostled for attention. Then, sooner or later, comes the moment when I experience recognition and know which way to go. I just needed to be patient and allow time. Over the years I have come to trust that the way will be illuminated and that there is no need to succumb to anxiety, even if sometimes I do.

I was attending the second Spirit in Business conference to be held in the US. I had been invited to present a workshop and I had called it 'The Circle of Fire'. It was an auspicious time for me, because I was looking for conferences and other events where I could begin to speak out more directly, moving forward my vision and undertaking what I consider to be my life's work. Two friends accompanied me: Dorota Ostoja Zawadzka, co-founder and director of our Polish company, Pathways Polska, and David Mann, who has stood by me for years now as I've slowly approached a more public platform. Pathways has existed in one form or another since 1989 – an 'organisation development consultancy', with most of our work focused around the twin themes of inspiration and leadership.

I was dreaming. I stood on a valley side looking out as far as my eyes would carry me. The colours of the land were those of autumn, and the land was folded in a countless series of ridges and valleys. There were small copses of trees, and occasional outcrops of rock. Tiny threads of silver laced the auburn sheen of distant combes, as small streams searched their way to a distant sea. The land was beautiful, somehow untouched, glowing with pride and integrity. Whichever way I looked I saw no sign of human habitation except way off to the north-west in the far distance, where I could just see the reflected roofs of a village. As I stood upon the hill I became aware of dusk. Light seemed to become absorbed into the grasses, trees, earth, and rock. As darkness embraced the land I became aware of moonlight and shadows that glided softly. Quite still, I drew the night around me and I waited. Unseen during the day, pulsing, silver, patterned and glowing, the faint outline of a path traced itself upon the land. Behind me the path reached back in time, curving, rising steeply, contouring around a hillside, fording a stream, describing a journey along the way I had come. Then as footprints on a frosty grassed field I saw how my own route had intertwined itself around that of the silver path. It looked like the footprints of a child who resists the relentless certainty of the long path ahead and seeks adventure by exploring the hidden mystery of the unknown. Sometimes it looked as if I had deliberately sought difficulty by choosing to fight my way through brambles, or stumble over rocks jagged with the frosts of many winters. In the footprints I could read the emotions of a thousand life experiences, the joys, the anger, the uncertainty, the wounded pride, the rage of injustice, the dogged steps of the weary, and the fierce pride of the young warrior. Like some great rule of law, the original rune that announced life, the path of grey silver glowed and pulsed, supremely confident, an invitation to the human, to me, yet carrying no judgement, no criticism.

Looking ahead again I understood that the path is only revealed at night, and that it is in the day that the journey must be made when the glowing handrail becomes invisible. At night, as we submit to sleep, we drink at the waters of the great well. We journey and travel, perhaps coming close to the dream that birthed us. Yet wherever we go during this time of sleeping most of us pay for the privilege with our memory. The renewal experienced through the blessing of sleep accepted and unquestioned. As the dream began to falter and fade I experienced a series of images flooding like water and shelving themselves for later inspection. I understood that the glowing pathway of my dream was my chosen destiny. It was a statement of intention made in a place and time that I cannot reach and no longer remember. I understood that the path was not a command, but a self-invitation, a graceful beckoning, a spiritual purpose. I understood that the path allowed and expected me to be self-responsible and make choices, and that in making choices I would sometimes lose my way. This path was not imposed by some external force, but was my own self-longing: a deep part of myself dreaming alive my most secret and sacred purpose. I understood that within each moment of each day I make choices that define who I am, and that I always possess the opportunity to correct foolish decisions. I understood that as I rise and stand at the beginning of each day I look out across a landscape of possibility, and that as I raise my foot and lean forward I declare myself to the world, and that life will surely receive my statement and respond appropriately. I understood that, no matter how far I might wander from the Invisible Path, it is always no more than one step away. That it is deeply magical, and will always strive to present itself to me. That it is in some way kind beyond knowing. I also understood that the path was not a statement of perfection, or that it precluded hard and challenging experience, simply that it described in symbolic form a way of being, a desire to be true to myself and walk my own way.

Others also walk the Invisible Path. If we were able to see the twin trails of all those who have walked their journey upon the dream land, we would see a landscape of vast breadth – a pattern that is the human experience on earth. We would witness journeys of extraordinary integrity and resolve. We would see unimaginable suffering. The suffering we would see would include the agony of the truly dispossessed, but there would also be countless millions of others whose faint heart has encouraged them to walk away from their true wisdom and seek fulfilment from false gods, whether this be in the arenas of work, religion, love, or the pursuit of happiness. My personal experience of stepping away from the Invisible Path, usually driven by the mindset of the rebellious adolescent, has led to the discovery of how painful it is to walk separated from life, from my own deeper intention. When I now stand again on that dream hillside and look back along the trail I have made, I see how perverse I have been in resisting my self-wisdom. I am amazed at how determined I have been to make difficulty for myself. Yet I also see that from the youngest age I desired to feel and experience life as fully as I could. I set my sights on goals that are largely considered redundant and fanciful in the culture and time in which I came to be born. If you wish to walk a long way, and if the journey is worth undertaking, then all must be risked, and none of us can insure against failure. It is risking everything that makes everything possible.

At 4.20 p.m. the MacBrayne ferry left Oban bound for Craignure on the Isle of Mull, off Scotland's west coast. I stood leaning against the ship rail with my arm around Azul's shoulders while Roman investigated what the ship had to offer by way of entertainment for an eleven-year-old boy. I let my eyes rest on the houses clustered along the quay, almost reluctant to look west and taste the new island world to which I was bound. I wanted to take my time and appreciate. Away to the west, south, and north were the cloud-shrouded isles of Scotland's ancient coastline and it felt thrilling to be stepping towards them at last. Mull was quiet, withdrawn, an island in deep introspection. We arrived at Fionnphort in the dark and rain. Glancing around, it felt it very unlikely that there was a bright fire anywhere close, a meal, and a warm bed. The wind was whipping up and a storm was forecast. A van clawed its way towards us. Our bags were flung in the back and we made a short and lumpy drive along a track to the jetty. Glen was waiting with a heavy-set open boat, engine running, and we turned into the night. The water was choppy and black and although the sea conditions were safe enough, there was, as there always is, a tension that accompanies boats at night in the sea as you search for the landfall. A wharf appeared ahead of us and the boat glided in the last few yards. We had arrived at the tiny isle of Erraid.

The bags were ferried up the steel stairs that clung to the sea-wall, and we hurried, heads down against the rain squalls, through the farm buildings towards the line of granite-walled cottages that sat hunched into the hillside. A door opened and warm air rushed to greet us. We had found the bright fire. This was an exploratory visit, a reconnaissance. A month or so later I would return, this time without Azul and Roman; just some books, a laptop computer, and a stack of hopes and fears.

I had been looking for a remote island cottage where I could spend two months, seeking to write the book that waited impatiently for my undivided attention. I almost went to Eigg instead. Alistair McIntosh's book Soil and Soul had brought me close to this island community and I felt, as I still do, that many of the issues of freedom, earth, spirit, and personal responsibility that inform Eigg's history are also mine. So when, prior to locating a cottage on Erraid, I found myself standing on Mallaig's harbour wall watching the Eigg ferry steam away without me on board, I was not happy. Together with a friend, we had raced from Edinburgh during the early hours, intent on our adventure. It was disappointing to find that with a gale coming in hard, we could sail to the island, but, having done so, we might find ourselves unable to return until the seas had calmed and the ferry resumed its habitual passage. With only a few days before the inaugural voyage of our own ship, we couldn't risk becoming marooned.

We left Mallaig and went on to the Kyle of Lochalsh where we were confronted with the Skye bridge toll and all the greed and self-interest that its recent history symbolises. It took us both by surprise when the woman in the tollbooth responded to our grudging payment with humour and generosity. We were disarmed and went over to Skye glad that we'd met her. A long day's driving and I still didn't have my cottage, so in the evening we came back across the bridge, this time with a bouquet of flowers for our friend. She had finished her shift and gone home so we left the flowers with a bemused colleague and set on, this time heading east.

I visited the Findhorn Foundation in the early 1980s, but, as the foundation began to adopt a more overtly new age Christian flavour to their spirituality, I never felt drawn to get closer. However, I had heard about the small community that was set up under the Findhorn Foundation's aegis at Erraid, and I liked the sound of it. Searching the Foundation's bookstore I found a leaflet introducing the Erraid community, noted the phone number and placed a call.

Coming across the strip of water that separates Erraid from Mull for the second occasion some months later, and this time to write, I felt quite different. Now the lines were drawn, and the blank page sat waiting. Acutely aware that I needed to start writing the next morning, I made my way to Cnoc Mor, Erraid's highest point, and introduced myself to the island. Looking out to Colonsay in the south, Soa to the west, and Iona almost close enough to touch in the north, I spoke about why I'd come and I asked for the island's blessing. I walked back to Pier Cottage, my home for December and January, gave some bread to the sparrows, went in and closed the door.

Seeking, stumbling, striding the Invisible Path, we describe a journey – and the journeys we make exist within landscapes that, while related, are often very different. We make intellectual journeys and experience all the hills and valleys that we might expect upon a physical journey. We make emotional journeys and may at times find ourselves bent double seeking breath, exhausted and doubting our resolve. We make physical journeys and amongst the heights of mountains find our thinking stimulated and enriched with powerful insights that move us forward. The best journeys for me are those that dance the four great powers of the physical, emotional, mental, and spiritual together – spun and woven as one cloth. The physical has been misunderstood, often despised, and mostly seen as being of less value than the spiritual, by people who claim to understand these things – 'spiritual' people. Such thinking endlessly reinforces the pre-eminence of hierarchy. It takes us away from the circle, and it separates us from ourselves. Whatever is in this book that is of value came from a touching, an intimate encounter with the powers of earth, water, air, and fire. The journey to Erraid and the two months I spent there were no different. Quietly, without obligation, the Invisible Path guided me to Erraid and, thankfully, I listened and accepted the invitation. On arrival I established one basic rule. I was on the isle to write, only this. So I wrote, and wrote, and wrote, eating my meals at the hospitable table of the Erraid community, sleeping sometimes, dreaming often, and walking every day. The walking was important. Sitting in front of my computer for hours on end was only made possible by the two hours of walking that were squeezed into each day. I expected to be nourished by these walks, but I never expected them to become so pivotal and central to the whole undertaking. Awake or asleep at all times of the day and night, driven by my writing, and walking every day in all weathers, I found in the island an elder, a relation of the oak tree from whom I had learnt many years previously. I felt my hand held snug in its wild fist, and I was graced with many insights that had meaning to me. For this reason I am including extracts from the journal that I kept during this time. The Erraid Journal traces a journey, the Invisible Path is itself a journey blessed with myriad paths, and this book is shaped around a journey. Journeys and stories sit well together. With all that is magical and wondrous in this world, journeys that become stories and stories that become journeys are among the most precious.

Isle of Erraid Journal – 1

THE COUNCIL OF THE ISLES

Erraid floats adrift on the rim of the world, an ancient galleon of the Celtic Sea, an island that when we sleep may slip her moorings and sail to some council held out there in the misted water-lands of the deep Atlantic. Silently she takes her place by the other isles for I fancy they are all Goddesses and Gods of the Aesir, faeries of the old woods, songs that are waiting for a singer. The island has scents of her own, sounds of her own, families of sparrows that stretch back over centuries and beyond. Her bays are sculpted by waves that have never ceased since water first kissed the shore. Erraid is old, 2,700 million years old, and therefore part of Britain's oldest rocks. Subject to six tectonic cycles, pressured, heated, thrown up by volcanoes in a ceremony of fire and smoke. Lava pouring from fissures beneath the boiling sea, erupting, fulfilling the dream of life, answering the call of creation. This is a land so close to spirit that songs and stories are always only one dream away. I stand by Cnoc Mor and look out to the four directions. I hear the pipes, I hear the voices raised around ancient fires, I fly with the ravens and I weep for the striving, for the dreaming, for the aching love that people have had for this wild and beautiful land.

So much blood flows in the burns and has soaked into the dark earth of the glens. So many tears have lodged in the peat of the people's fires. Up until a very short while ago the Highland clearances were never spoken of. Neither was Gaelic. It was forbidden. Take away a people's language, bury their history, break their customs, school the children in slavery: all this was the strategy of England's Lords, and they did their job thoroughly. Even many of the Highlanders' own chiefs betrayed the people. Then they

Erraid: the western shore

romanticised it all and tartan was born. Back to Scotland was given a sentimentalised version of something that had once been real, something that had possessed life. No life, not any more, or so it seemed for a while. It is not to the south that the Scots should look when the children are told of how this land was blighted. The English people were subject to the same tyranny. When we allowed the few to take the land from under our feet, to appoint themselves our lords, and hold us imprisoned in the pursuit of their wealth and their self-aggrandisement, when we bought into the whole ridiculous charade of ever-increasing wealth, and a life in which we no longer know who we are, we lost ourselves and forgot we ever felt different. We have all felt the weight. Even now in the 21st century we are 'subjects'. Yet the dragon has life in it yet. St George didn't finish the job. These islands are still the home place of freedom fighters like Thomas Paine, and nothing is finished until it is finished.

What is it that Erraid and Iona, Skye and Mull, Harris and Lewis, and all the other isles council about when they meet while we are asleep? They become the songs that they are, and they dream tomorrow. They whisper courage into the ear of the sleeping young girl child, and they breathe a wind amongst the people that we notice as an idea, and the idea is the knowledge that we can have … everything. Even our cake.

That we do not have dreams for nothing.

That the Invisible Path will never betray us, and that love is the power that gave us the joy of choice.

That we can choose to build beauty in our lives, and that we can die proud.

I shall go to bed early tonight for I would not wish to delay their meeting.

The garden has been with me forever. As a child it was my whole world and now, at 57 years, it is the ground I stand upon. In many ways very little has changed. When I was five I used to gulp my breakfast down and run outside, intoxicated with the mystery of what might be discovered. One of the greatest gifts my mother and father gave their three children was a portion of the garden as our very own. Here we dug tunnels, built dens, hoarded treasures and fought great battles. The 'Little Corner', as it was known by the family, was located on the garden boundary and shaded by an enormous Japanese Oak tree. I must have spent hundreds of hours playing under the shelter of this magnificent tree, and now as I reflect on those years the tree assumes even greater significance – a mentor, silent, vast in spirit and wisdom. We gathered great armfuls of autumn leaves and threw them at each other. We stuffed old clothes with them and created enemies whom we could always beat. We gathered bags of acorns and felt rich. We stared in awe at the gigantic limbs reaching out above us and dreamed of being able to climb such a tree. There were other trees as well. Lime trees which had once been pruned so that the branches stretched out horizontally to connect with those of the next tree. We could climb from one tree to the next. The garden was also an orchard and as children we knew each tree intimately – its smell, bark, fruit, leaves, branches and climbing routes. I have loved trees ever since. The garden is a school, for children and for adults. Here we can exercise imagination, learn to use tools, build shelters, solve problems, climb trees, argue, negotiate, laugh and cry. We learn the smell of earth and the difference between soil and dirt. What effectively destroys a garden is the adults' strange desire to make it clean in the same way as a house is made clean. Over recent years we have imported the garden into our houses – generally to their benefit, but we also seem to have exported the house into our gardens – generally to their detriment. This usually means that there are more objects than plants, very little earth, nothing out of place, and a stifling sense of relentless control. I also learnt that gardens grow food, lots of food. This impressed me and my respect grew alongside the potatoes, leeks and onions. Most of all, the garden taught me reverence for our earth, and the deep understanding that I am connected to her, inseparable, a part of life. This has never left me.

I grew up loving trees, earth, meadow-grass, rivers, streams and sky with a passion as strong now as ever. I understood nothing except that I loved these things and that they were precious to me beyond imagining. Bad weather was meaningless to me except that it provided new impetus to our games. If it was raining, we were awaiting the great flood; if it was sunny, we were staggering across the desert dying with thirst; the first hint of snow and the garden became the Yukon in 1880. It was a feast and I sat at this table every day. Within walking distance of the garden was the incomparable joy of 2,400 acres of undeveloped parkland, Sutton Park. There were swamps, lakes, meadows, impenetrable woods, big stretches of rough grazing, heath, tracks, rabbit warrens, foxes, everything I loved.

At a certain place in Sutton Park there is a holly tree of great significance. I haven't been there for some years so it may be quite a substantial tree by now, although holly does not hasten to maturity and I don't remember it changing that much over the years we used to visit it. There are many holly trees in Sutton Park, but as far as I am aware it is only under this particular one that there is treasure. I know, because we put it there. I think it was my father's inspiration that first conceived this idea. We got a jamjar and put an assortment of treasures into it, like halfpennies, threepenny pieces, marbles, and messages. Other things went in too, crayons, acorns, badges, and then our small family group ventured into the park and selected the tree. Holly is prickly and therefore discourages would-be thieves randomly moving across the park hunting under trees for treasure. So it seemed to be a good choice of hiding place. To further safeguard the treasure we maintained guard while nonchalantly approaching the tree and then burrowing under it and secreting the jamjar. It was a very tense and intense exercise, and we loved it. Periodically over the years we would set out on expeditions to rediscover our treasure. In a fever of excitement, speculating on the likelihood of success, and desperately trying to remember what the treasure was composed of, we would launch out from the house and set forth. Each time we found the jamjar it would bring the same electrifying excitement, both in the search and in the moment of truth as the lid was unscrewed.

The garden was always a place of deep mystery and beauty for me. It held the promise of treasure. It taught me about value and ultimately about values. The garden has the capacity to teach us about creation because this is what it is. Even in the most tyrannically suppressed garden there exist millions of life forms, and it is from plants, animals, the earth, that we construct our unconscious appreciation of beauty. Just as we mostly forget the dreams given us during the dark of sleep, we also forget the treasure buried in the gardens of our younger years. All children, given the chance, understand the joy of grass, sky, trees and rocks. Unless already hurt and damaged themselves they instinctively care for animals. As children we readily inculcate an understanding of ecology and the values of sustainability. But if, as we grow older, we learn that such things are the domain of the childish and immature, we will leave them behind as fast as we can clutch an understanding of what it is that represents the 'real' world. Then comes our first autumn and the leaves fall. Our treasure is obscured – gentled amongst the fronds and flowers of the garden and held safe should we ever return to find it. With the passage of time the treasure becomes more deeply hidden and, with more time still, it may succumb to decay. Even then there will exist the memory, a footprint lightly traced upon the invisible.

By the time we are adult we have treasure buried in many gardens.

CHAPTER TWO

The garden growing

For my brothers and me, Robin Hood was a true hero. We played endless games devoted to the enactment of his adventures, and our father's workshop regularly used to ring to the sound of inexpert carpenters smashing together another set of armour. Double-handed swords, staves, ridiculously heavy nail-studded shields, and bows that were genuinely lethal, all were manufactured with focused concentration and absolute commitment to the principles of good weaponry. If, on the infrequent occasions we watched TV, there was a serialisation that made any mention of Robin Hood, we soaked it up, hungry and uncritical acolytes. For weeks and months afterwards the garden would resound to the shouts and screams of the victor and the vanquished. On one occasion my elder brother, James, had been very impressed by Robin's resourcefulness in attending to his stricken comrade, Little John, by massaging salt into an open wound that John had endured in Robin's defence. I'm surprised that John didn't kill him for this barbaric ministration, but in fact he just grimaced, tensed, and buttoned his shirt again. So when I fell out of one of the trees in our garden and raked my back on a nail that was protruding from the trunk, James seized the opportunity to do the right thing and raced to the house for the salt. It was an impressive wound, about nine inches long. To the dispassionate observer it may have appeared more like a bad scratch, but in my imagination the nail had narrowly avoided slicing through my heart as it gouged its way through muscle, tissue and bone. Waiting for medical attention, I was consoled by the thought that I might have a very large and livid scar as permanent testimony. We valued scars highly. James returned with the salt and, like John, I was advised to bite on something while he applied the remedy ... In later life I was not surprised when he chose to train in the medical profession as a pathologist.

Davy Crockett, as served up by Walt Disney, was another childhood hero. Both men were leaders working outside the establishment, both upheld justice, both placed integrity, freedom, bravery and service ahead of their own comfort and self-interest, and both showed a reckless indifference to their own safety or that of others. I was very impressed. Whether or not today's two-dimensional characters in films and stories bear any resemblance to the originators of these folk myths I rather doubt, but along with others they burned their indelible imprint upon my childish imagination. I don't know how much time Davy spent in deep forest country hobnobbing with Indian friends, if indeed he had any, and certainly today neither Tennessee nor the Alamo in Texas are famed for their lush green woodlands. In my mind it was different and the Tennessee my younger brother and I inhabited was above all leafy. It was deeply mysterious. It was ancient, and it called to my heart. The love affairs of our youngest years speak deeply to us. We are influenced and I think we make choices. Somewhere within me I fell in love with the garden that was gifted to me in those early years. I didn't know that it was already polluted, already in decline. I just knew that I loved the sights, sounds, scents and textures of earth, sun, wind, and water – of plants and animals. My mythical Robin Hood and Davy Crockett served to illustrate humans within the world of nature, inextricably bound to and part of all things. Not alien, but moving in sympathy with the environment that had birthed them. They made me a gift of incalculable value. Our games were not peaceful. Bristling with weapons, we waged endless bloody wars beneath the canopy of green that sheltered our learning. Forever cut, scratched, bruised and dirty, we drew to us the deep love that trees and grass represent, and we were stricken. There is no going back once held in this embrace. The guns, the bows, the violence and the aggression are not what they seem. We were pups. We fought and postured. We endlessly argued. We made friends, became enemies, and then returned to friendship a minute or two later. We practised being human, we experimented. We explored issues of power, compassion, meanness and generosity, and we began the long journey of finding out who we were.

As a child I loved constructing chambers under the ground. With my brothers we would dig a system of trenches, deep and wide enough to crawl along, with different rooms and antechambers. It was hard work shifting all that soil but we loved it and no amount of effort was too much. When the trenches had been excavated we placed wood rafters across the tunnels and then covered these with corrugated iron sheeting of which we had a plentiful supply. Onto the sheeting went the soil again, and then finally it was dressed as naturally as we could make it, so that the casual passer-by might not guess that beneath the surface was a system of secret tunnels. The excitement of first entering newly made tunnels was intense. They had to be checked for light, for we wanted them pitch black; then we added various modifications and improvements, such as creating sleeping quarters, food storage etc. Endless games were played in these tunnels, but it was particularly exciting to go down into them at night with candles, open the trapdoor and disappear into the earth. One particular evening we had done just this and were inside the tunnel system enjoying ourselves, when a somewhat nervous, agitated voice called out: 'Who's there? Come on out!' Already escaping from a prisoner-of-war camp and deep inside enemy territory, this sudden interruption seemed entirely in keeping with the world we inhabited and it took us a while to separate the two. Eventually, with a few more tense exhortations from the adult voice outside, we eased the trapdoor open a fraction and a powerful torch beam swivelled to meet us.

'What are you doing?' demanded the voice.

'Playing', one of us said simply. There was a pause while this information was digested. We could sense that the voice was struggling for the next question. It gave up and instead issued a command.

'Come on out.' One by one, glancing at each other in the distorted shifting light of the torch, we emerged from the tunnel, smudged and grimy. I don't remember being encouraged to find that the voice belonged to a policeman. He was standing on the other side of our garden fence in a small lane that followed our boundary. Fulfilling his pledge to Queen and country he had, of course, sought to unravel this suspicious circumstance and set the world back to rights. This he did and we lived to continue our love affair with dark earth.

Learning is not always kind. At one time I was visiting a friend of mine near Malvern where I was born. We were of a similar age, at that time about nine or ten. My friend, Richard, had an air rifle and we decided to go hunting. It was one of those mornings when everything was perfect, the excitement of the day's plans, the smell of breakfast wafting up the stairs, bright sunlight streaming through the gaps between curtains, and outside a cacophony of birdsong. The rifle made us both feel very powerful. It smelt of gun oil, wood and adventure. Our imaginations brimmed with images of grizzly bears, moose and elk. The talk was tough, uncompromising. Once outside our game gained pace and a sense of urgency began to take over. We were eager for the kill. Almost before I knew it we were crouched below one of the garden walls and searching for our prey. He came within minutes, a tiny bundle of beauty, a robin. As the rifle was swung to Richard's shoulder and his cheek pressed to the wooden stock I had my first vague sense of doubt, but the power we wielded was strong and there was no going back for either of us. We tensed, the bird presented his profile, head tilted and questioning. A finger squeezed and with the crack of the shot we watched as the robin was hurled backwards, instantly dead. We stepped forward and studied our work. I have not forgotten the sense of guilt and sadness, a vacuum of loneliness. The knowledge that we had done something very wrong – that I had known it was wrong all along, but I hadn't spoken up. I wanted that feeling of power. A couple of years later I almost repeated this act but in an even more premeditated act. I sprinkled bread on the lawn at the back of our house and then climbed a tree with my rifle. As the birds came to eat I took two shots. I missed on both. I knew that if I waited the birds would return in just a few minutes, but the sickness of my heart became too much and I climbed back down the tree never to do the same again.

There is much that is written about the formative years of childhood, particularly as it relates to parents and siblings – far less about other relationships equally important and pivotal in our balanced development as creative, sensitive, and fulfilled adults. It is a matter of utmost concern for our longevity as a species and the quality of our individual and collective lives that we learn to appreciate that we owe everything to *the earth* that birthed us. Without this we are disconnected from life and grow up with all the imbalances of the unloved orphan forever searching for love through possession and control. Without strong affective bonds we seek a relationship with our world by living out the fear and distress of our abandonment. Without the deep knowledge of belonging we work out our anger, taking savage swipes at our betrayer. If we do not come to understand the true and vast value of air, trees, sunlight and the many beings with whom we share space, we will of course behave and act as if they were expendable. We can name gods to our heart's content, but if they shift our attention away from the profound mystery of our familial relationship with nature, they do us no good service. She is the centre. The universe reaches out and Earth gets smaller. Her centrality is challenged. But for the young child the mother is always the centre, and we are, if nothing else, forever young.

The second relationship is with our *imagination*. There can be no adult without imagination, and certainly no leader. At best there can only be a bureaucrat. In imagination we have a gift capable of returning us to the stars while sitting on the banks of a pristine highland tarn and loving, valuing, appreciating both. We can fill our nostrils with the scent of hay warming in the sun while traversing the universe or comforting a friend sat on the other side of the world. Many of us never grow a confident relationship with our imagination. It is stifled and controlled by tramlines of different kinds and we become dependent on the dreams of others, and part of what makes us human withers.

The relationship we have with our earth and the relationship we have with our imagination – they also need to come together in relationship. Whatever we build in life is driven by our imagination and if we have not found the relationships that demonstrate the web of interconnectedness that is life, then again we develop a separation between heart and head – the gulf separating the life sciences from the physical sciences.

I experienced many times of great joy as a child, but I was in no way adequately prepared when I unwittingly walked into my first sustained period of real challenge. During this time I had to fight for every scrap of self-knowledge, and every foothold of self-worth. I began a kind of apprenticeship and the task of bringing my dreams into relationship with the culture and times into which I had been born. I am not amongst those, therefore, that hanker after the days of their childhood or youth. It seems to me that life is ever more generous in her yielding. Yet I don't wish away the past either. Every scar and bruise, the blazing wonder of friendships, the scent of rain on warm earth, and the ecstasy of waking to the first day of the summer holidays. These I treasure, holding each close to the hearth fire of my remembering. With them I also treasure struggles with ill health, crushed hopes, the toxic fear that threatened to engulf me on the eve of many battles, the long dark times when I believed I was lost to myself. There is no teacher like life experience, and without the abrasion of trial we cannot find measure. What is best of all now is the knowledge that whatever has been won or lost during my time, Ragnarok is not yet fought, and in the waiting I have found who I truly am.

The journey that a child takes towards knowing her- or himself is a tough one. Almost nothing in my education even acknowledged that this was important. Libraries are crammed with information, the internet groans under its vast virtual weight, but it is the passion and imagination of humans that then use this information to create and build self-knowing. Some years ago I returned to Warwick School to see how the monster I shared ten years of my life with was faring. It was bewildering to observe that it looked almost normal, even … fun. In fact my last few years at this school were markedly different from the preceding seven. The old guard had left on the last train, gone forever. Even now it is hard not to hope that they shared some measure of the cruelty they so casually dispensed.

I was nine and a half when I first arrived outside the gates of Warwick School. It was 1958. On an unimaginably dark January night my parents drove me to the place I was to spend the next ten years. Boarding school had not been part of the plan but my spectacularly poor academic performance had confronted my parents with a problem, and this was the solution. Shortly before leaving, my father gave me his car key ring. It sported the logo of the National Benzol Mixture company, and I had always admired it. Whatever shred of self-control I had clung to now evaporated, and for the first time I knew the pain of separating from loved ones. His gift felt like an act of supreme self-sacrifice and it touched me to the core. Somewhere inside I knew he did it because he couldn't find the words. My mother was always easier with emotion, and I felt her love as a robe of care wrapped around my shoulders. A short while later they departed and I walked towards the dormitory. I could hear the screaming some way off. Ellis Trowe's trousers were round his ankles and efforts were being made to lift him off the floor by his penis. His bed was next to mine. Each morning he would be woken by a hail of heavy leather-soled school shoes, sometimes metal-tipped. Each morning he would see the light of day through a veil of tears. Another child who arrived some time later was forced to travel the entire length of the dining room under the tables to fetch sugar for one of the senior boys – every morning for weeks. He was kicked savagely the whole length of the way. Not long after, William Sears arrived. King Will as he came to be known. With him came a reign of terror that is still remembered by those that were there. Later, as an adult, I heard that King Will blew his brains out in some hotel room. The child who had now become a senior executive in the BBC gave me this news some years ago. His faced was creased and cold with hatred. 'I don't give a fuck', he said, 'I hate him still'. Another two of our crowd attempted suicide as adults. One of them succeeded. Another went to prison for VAT fraud. Many left with wounds to heal. I have been asked why much of this was never told at the time to teachers who might have taken action to protect us. Like the law that exists in our prisons, when at some point the teachers' doors close and you walk back into the jungle, you walk alone. We were none of us that stupid.

The junior boarding house was the worst, and it had a suitably brutal housemaster. Mr Dunnal personally took it upon himself to apply the corrective treatment that 'Jelly' Vorster needed to make him a man, and I wonder if Jelly still has the scars to prove it. Mr Dunnal's dogged persistence in the light of Jelly's intransigence was impressive. He never gave up, and Jelly learnt what it is to live with terror. We all tasted Dunnal's cane. Since the caning often happened when we were wearing our pyjamas, the tears that would be unwillingly squeezed from between tightly clenched eyelids would be matched by fat droplets of blood staining our buttocks.

In all of this, and of course there is much, much more, there was always a core of hope. We were children, and we could take a lot. The friendships of that time were strong and for those that were physically talented there was always sport. We lived, ate, and breathed sport. In this, if only briefly, we became powerful. When asthma arrived I was devastated. I had settled into the cosy familiarity of consistently achieving the dubious distinction of being twenty-fourth out of twenty-five in the D stream. There was no-one below me, and only one of my mates as company at twenty-fourth equal. To occupy such a place in the spirit of rebellion, implying that if I cared enough I could do better, was manageable only because I excelled in the gymnasium, on the rugby field, and appeared tough. Removing all of this left me with nothing and gulping on an inhaler filled me with shame, crushing my spirit.

It seems we have to get lost in order to become interested in questions of location and navigation.

Days passed by smoothly enough, but underneath I was in grief. In the early days while Ellis Trowe endured his education at the hands of his classmates I spotted an avenue whereby I could perhaps avoid the chill privilege of being the only new boy to arrive during the appropriately named 'Lent' term. Boys, even those caught in their own version of William Golding's *Lord of the Flies*, enjoy stories, and I told stories like none other. Night after night I burrowed into the imaginal and knelt before the Muse pleading my case for a story with which to hold back the less welcome attention of idle minds. I fabricated an entire history, an entire life. I would sit propped up in bed in the half gloom of C dormitory, acutely aware of my rapt audience-weaving tales of a childhood in Africa. I turned myself into some kind of Mowgli figure from Rudyard Kipling's *The Jungle Book*, shifted continents to get more scope for large and dangerous animals, granted myself parents who appeared to allow their son to roam wild and free across the Serengeti, and learnt very fast how to survive – in C dormitory of Warwick School. I had a pet rock python, sixty feet in length, and could string out a good death scene over an hour or more. I was tortured by natives, boiled in a pot, and ran for days on end without water across landscapes more barren than the Moon. I hinted at a telepathic relationship with animals, an acute sensitivity to the forest, and the trees. I claimed that if a friend of mine spoke in genuine need, even though I might be several hundred miles away, the wind would bring me their words and I would hear them, and I would come as the avenger of all wrongs. I claimed prodigious strength when angered and a pitiless viciousness when exacting revenge. I carefully shaped my character as one who would prefer to co-operate and be genial, but who also had a taste for savage reprisal if wronged. I used and learnt every skill I could in working the propaganda that might keep me safe, and, after a fashion, it worked.

So when asthma came around the time of my fourteenth birthday I turned to the same place inside myself, and dreamed a different dream. Only this time I think the trees did hear me, and the wind passed the message on to the place where lives are woven and spun. In the summer term when I was fifteen years old I used to sit by a very small, young and delicate cherry tree that grew way out in the school playing fields. Here I wrote poems – passionate confused verse that tore at the future and invoked a world I believed lost. Lonely and unhappy I poured out my longing and sought to place the tiny truth of my present life within the landscape I yearned to one day inhabit. The trouble was, everyone around me told me that it no longer existed – maybe never did. The pain of this was big. I loved the trees, I loved the games of imagination I created, I loved the river Arrow that I used to swim in at Jonney Haddams' farm. I loved the Sun. All these wondrous things I loved, and I could not bear to be parted from them. Yet all of this was childish and not real. I could see nothing of any value in the adult world that beckoned. So I grew up slowly until I was ready.

Working with leaders in organisations I have become aware of how powerfully stories govern our behaviour and serve unconscious needs. Internalised myths are told and retold within the circle of our own private contemplation. Simplistic and idealised versions of 'self' are promulgated within the psyche of most leaders and upon these we lean, lightly or heavily. Described in such a way these inner stories may seem delusional, and so they may be, but they can also serve to remind us of treasure buried under a holly tree some years past when the world was less threatening.

When Kit Whitten left Warwick School he made his way to Portsmouth where he continued his education. By the time he left the school he had become in large part, a reformed character. However, I suspect that there was still a collective sigh of relief from the school's teaching fraternity as his mother bundled him off the premises for the last time. He had a great sense of humour and beneath the glowering exterior there lurked a formidable intelligence, but for some reason he chose to slum it with the rest of us in the lower echelons of the school's academic hierarchy. What made him different was his capacity for aggression and sudden acts of shocking savagery, the like of which had rarely been seen, even at Warwick School. On one occasion he deliberately and overtly attacked one of the teachers during a 'friendly' football match. With ruthless precision he drop-kicked the man in the throat and then with each of his 196lbs stamped on his abdomen. For this he was cautioned. He was, beyond doubt, dangerous and out of control. By the time he was eleven Kit looked terrifying in school uniform. There was something absurdly intimidating about shorts and a blazer when the person in it looked more like a stevedore from a dock in London's East End. By the time he was eighteen our 1st Fifteen rugby team was massively enhanced by his ability to inspire fear into the ranks of the opposition. He was the tight head prop forward and I was the hooker. On my left was Galbraith. Galbraith was an enormously strong gentle giant. There was nothing bad about Galbraith. All that was with Kit and me, but Kit was a good deal more able to wield it to our advantage. At this time Bablake School had a formidable and very nasty prop forward themselves. I never knew his name but he was both very powerful and sadistic. During one match, unseen by the referee, who was probably inured to extremes of mindless violence, this character began to destroy Galbraith by repeatedly smashing his fist into Galbraith's unprotected face. In true form, Galbraith did not respond but passively and mightily exerted his vast strength legally and professionally, against his opponent. With each scrummage the punches continued and Galbraith became drenched in blood. Finally after frequent exhortations from myself, Kit, irritated at having his game interrupted, clapped a hairy hand on Galbraith's shoulder and signalled him to swap to the other side. There was a look of smug satisfaction on the Bablake prop's face as he swung to face his new foe, but I swear I saw his face drain white as he saw the expression on Kit's face. Deep in the scrum I turned my face away. I knew it would be horrible. There was a pause and then a kind of disembodied shrieking began to quaver through the pack. A terrible thought flickered through my mind as I imagined our first ever fatality on the rugby pitch, followed by a cynical fantasy based on whether the Headmaster would consider this cause for celebration or retribution. The body in front and to my left was now jerking convulsively. He went down like a stone and the whole Warwick pack stamped him into the mud.

It was, I suppose, allegorical, a kind of life training, a ritual pageant in the chivalric tradition. I don't recollect that we spent much time reflecting on the school motto Altiora Peto ('I strive for higher things'), but if we had, it might have provided us with rich and no doubt troubling contradictions. Outside of blatantly hypocritical platitudes, we were left to ourselves when working out personal values and their relationship with wider society mores.

I never succeeded in learning much from my school lessons, but with living I learned well...

I learned that injustice is endemic and is usually made acceptable by being carefully ensconced inside tradition.

I learned that all people respond to stories that elevate the human spirit and appeal to our deeper sensibilities.

I learned that without courage and without risk life will pass like sand between our fingers.

I learned that the wild places, the animals, the clouds and the small streams have in them a magic that can heal and comfort.

I learned that friends, true friends, are more powerful than the worst enemy and more valuable than almost anything.

I learned that persistence, the absolute determination never to give up, never to lose hope, never to succumb to cynicism, will always eventually lead to attainment.

I learned that nothing is worse or more dangerous to a man or the world he inhabits than believing beauty to be anything less than a goddess.

I learned that I did not have to participate in a world of mortgages, pensions, cars, tedious work and bored relationships.

I learned that in giving we do truly receive, and that to belong we must serve something bigger than ourselves.

I learned that the worst slavery exists in people's minds and their unwillingness to be self-critical.

I learned that I could have adventure, could love beautiful women, could love children, could find meaning, fulfilment, and joy.

... If, if, if, if, if ... I cut away the anchor, swung the tiller over, drove hard on the wind, hauled tight the sheets, and took a course for the unknown.

I was once told, 'You take one step towards life, and she will take ten towards you'.

It is true.

Volharding off the Essex coast before heading north
to Crinan on the west coast of Scotland

Isle of Erraid Journal – 2

The island of Erraid, one mile by one mile, sounds a very small space but it isn't. There are hidden valleys, places where secrets have been stored, where pledges are still whispered to the stones. A mysterious place, ancient and sacred. Bog myrtle, marsh grass, bracken, all manner of different ferns and moss. The isle is rich. It is Prospero's isle. Willow, Silver Birch, Aspen, Oak, even with sheep the trees hold on. Each day I'd walk out and explore, and spend time with the island and listen to her.

It is very strange how we describe our land. Adjectives which talk of a cruel frost, a heartless winter, depressing rain, unforgiving soil etc. ... Yet would it not be truer to describe ourselves in this way? Did nature deforest huge swathes of forest in Spain, turning a garden into the poor stricken waterless land so much of Spain now is? Where did the soil go that used to grow the tall grass of Tennessee? Was that nature's cruelty? We demonstrate the same kind of insanity when we describe animals in this way: loving dogs while hating cats, or the other way around. Cherishing blue tits while hating magpies, slugs, foxes. Vermin. We even do it with plants, reserving our worst for anything that fights back: nettles, ivy, brambles, docks. Weeds. We don't have to hate in order to eat, build our homes, or grow our gardens. We are all becoming aware of the many plants growing in the rainforest that have medicinal properties, but one day I think we'll realise that all plants heal, and that all shelter life, provide life, and nourish life. We will still assist the plants we want to grow by hoeing out others, but we won't try to eliminate them, and we may even apologise from time to time, if we're wise.

Do we want children to find worms disgusting, children who can't bear to pick up a spider because they've been taught to find them repulsive? We take the wild places and we make a thing that is sweet and sugary, sentimental, untrue and false, and then serve it to our children in the form of cartoons. At this time when we know that the science of ecology and the revelations of cosmology are vital to our own well-being and survival as a species, we exclude most of this information from our children's education. In fact we highlight our contempt for it by including elements of environmental education when they are young, and then ignoring it when they are older. What we teach children to value remains with them all their lives. What we exclude they notice subliminally. What we reward is absorbed and converted to values. Young people challenge and confront received wisdom. This is what they are meant to do, but if what we taught them had integrity then it would not be rejected out of hand. Our young people are bright enough to discern the true from the untrue if they are given unbiased information. As it is, many reject the vacuous cynicism of our contemporary society while remaining trapped in it. So they get stoned and make themselves numb. We must teach them something that they can be inspired by.

We are uneasy with concepts like destiny. They take us uncomfortably close to fate, and from this we recoil. They lead us to an ancient world, disturbing, shadowed, and archaic. They lead us to the wild wood, but we have long since forgotten the old paths that would guide us on our way. Yet destiny exists and lives still. There was an inevitability in the passage I made once released upon the world as a young man. At that time I didn't realise the unity that exists between the outer and inner life. I didn't understand that the tensions, the unresolved, the dynamic interplay of unconscious forces wrestling for control, would inevitably steer me to experiences guiding me towards self-understanding. As children we believe that once we've found release from parental domination we will at last be free to create our lives as we wish and find happiness. For some, perhaps it is that simple. For many others, there is a dawning realisation that with freedom comes self-responsibility, and less tangible scapegoats upon whom to unleash our frustrations. Everything that lives unconscious within us has a disproportionately powerful effect in shaping our adult lives. We are led by the nose, as it were. Situations are somehow constructed in which we come face to face with forces whose existence we only know from fairy stories. And we gain life experience. Whatever is unconscious in an individual will find expression – one way or another. Although sometimes excruciatingly painful, life experience gives us the opportunity to become acquainted with what lurks below the grey waves. We do not have to make enemies of ourselves by attempting to banish dimensions of our psyche that do not fit within our preferred self-image even if they often assume monstrous proportions on first meeting. We can befriend ourselves and seek healing. Jung wrote:

> What happens to a person is characteristic of him. He
> represents a pattern and all the pieces fit. One by one, as his
> life proceeds, they fall into place according to some
> predestined design.*

It is as if a great mirror is held up to us and we are invited to take a look at the truths reflected there. It takes courage to gaze into the mirror.

Somewhere deep within a prayer had been born inside me as I grew up. It was like a small fire, smouldering, waiting its time, latent and holding an intent that was all the more intense for its containment. When something inside us becomes committed to the Invisible Path – our path of destiny, no matter if this remains largely dormant and unexpressed – events take on an accelerated motion in direct response to the internal yearning. As a young man shaking off his years of

* C.G. Jung, *Psychological Reflections* (ed. Jolande Jacobi), Routledge & Kegan Paul, London, 1971, p. 322.

incarceration I assumed that my life would now be free of irritating restrictions and that I could now get on with ... with whatever it was I was going to do. So I stepped away from Warwick School and, ignoring whatever portents or signs that presented themselves, I made my way to Loughborough College to train as a physical education teacher. I was buying time really. Once my asthma had been brought under control, sport was my salvation during schooldays, but it was fast losing its appeal as I began to glimpse how broad the horizon was becoming. Within days of arriving at Loughborough I had discovered educational drama and my heart was won over. Not only my heart. Like most young men I had only one thing on my mind, and the almost exclusively female population of the drama group did not pass my notice. Beyond this, other forces were at work. Without knowing it I was finding my way back to the imaginal, to the garden of my childhood. Briefly, I felt on track. It helps a lot if you have at least an inkling that the Invisible Path exists. You may not see it, you may not even feel it, but if somewhere between wakefulness and sleep you catch a glimpse of destiny hovering, it is above all else comforting. This is how it was for me. I had made her acquaintance too often in younger days – felt her breath upon my cheek, known her caress, and smelt the scent upon her gown. Drama took me back to the garden and physical education became irrelevant, except in so far as it led me back to rivers and mountains – to the gods and goddesses of all spiritual experience.

Drugs have been around forever, but as I came to manhood in the sixties they became the mantra of our age. At this time they possessed a mystery and allure that has now long since evaporated. If you were adventurous, spiritually inquisitive, critical of the status quo, idealistic and naive, you were going to take drugs. It was never going to be enough for me to walk a cliff edge physically. My spiritually embryonic longings had been baptised in the religion of Wesley and Calvin. To exit and walk my own way I first needed to enter the territory of Baudelaire and Neruda to acknowledge the deeply sensuous, sexually charged, physically potent young man that I was, and comprehend that all this is contained and celebrated within the love that birthed creation.

During my first term at Loughborough College I went down to see Kit in Portsmouth. He was doing a course in business studies, which he later employed to great effect in Brixton.

It was hard for many of us to understand each other at this time because the jargon of the peace generation was now flowing thick and fast, and changing by the day. Kit, I now discovered, had become a hippy. Where a public school education had failed, chemicals were doing the job. He was very cool, and affable. The aura of violence that had once held so many in thrall was now all but gone. We had a great time on the hill above Portsmouth, chatting about what we now considered as the old times, and contemplating our career prospects. Drugs was all the talk in the media and, of course, in our music. I was curious, uninformed, and after a chance encounter during a Hendrix concert with a man at Woburn Abbey who was lying in the urinals picking scabs off his arms with a syringe, I had become decidedly paranoid about the whole issue. I think I was quite confused. At about midnight Kit asked me if I was ready to "crash out". I stared wildly at him, and too loudly and too quickly said that I certainly wasn't ready for that yet. We knew each other very well, having spent the last ten years incarcerated in the same cell, but he didn't register any surprise and the evening continued. He was however, clearly very tired. By 2 a.m. he looked a little haggard. Again he asked me if I would be crashing out soon. I'd already spent the last two hours in deep turmoil trying to reconcile myself to the fact that my friend was a junkie, and that if I wasn't careful he'd take me with him.

"No!" I said with rather more force than he clearly thought was necessary. By this time I was very deeply tired and Kit looked the same, but I wanted to remain fully alert just in case. Finally, Kit stood, and dragging himself to his tent commented that he really did have to crash out. Hair vertical on the back of my neck, I waited, and waited, until a slow dawning relief engulfed me and I realised that "crashing out" was going to sleep.

It was good to be outside and walking on a mountain that I had often admired from the A5 road as I came along the Nant Gwynant Pass to or from Bangor in North Wales. Yr Garn has folds and rock outcrops that had always appealed to my eye and although it is steep I fancied I could be up to the top in an hour or so. It was late summer and already the scent of autumn was signalling the change of season. Sunlight washed against the hillsides and the aroma specific to these hills filled my nostrils with delight. I was very fit, enjoying the strength and power of a body that had been rigorously exercised all my life. I flung myself to the mountain and happily anticipated the stretch and pull of pushing myself on the curving upward path. In those days I didn't much concern myself with conserving energy. I had it to burn, and I exalted in the mountain's invitation.

About halfway I gradually became aware of something wrong. Unaccountably my strength seemed to be bleeding away. What should have been an easy, if strenuous, walk was causing me real difficulties. I shrugged it off, thinking that I just hadn't warmed up yet. An implausible reason since I had never really bothered with warming up anyway. I struck on, and the bright sunshine and verdant green hillsides seemed to mock my tortuous and labouring ascent. Asthma was still a condition that I lived with; and unless I had a cold I would only have to use the inhaler once and then I'd usually be able to undertake any kind of strenuous physical work without hindrance. Although my breathing seemed normal I stopped and dug out the inhaler. It was more an opportunity to stop and rest, but I needed an excuse. Deep inside I was worried and very confused. Nothing had ever felt like this, before or after. It was as if I had lead plates strapped to my legs and torso. The simplest of moves demanded the most extreme effort, and it was getting worse. I struggled on. It was now at least two hours since I had left the car and I still had the steepest section ahead of me. I became very engrossed in my own introspection. It felt as if a great weight – I hesitate to say premonition – had descended upon me. I felt a kind of internal oppression, as if a dark cloud had penetrated inside me and was gnawing at my guts. The exuberant mood that had led me to grab my boots and dash for the mountain was long gone. As I stumbled on I became as remorseless in my determination to reach the top as the condition which now threatened my success. The last section was debilitating. When I finally crested the summit I had to sink to the ground and close my eyes. The clouds skimmed the peaks and cloud shadows hunted amongst the cwms. A raven cawed and another responded. I lay quite still wondering if I was ill, bewildered, routed.

The journey back down was uneventful. I concentrated on maintaining balance as I negotiated the scree paths and the sheep tracks of the lower slopes. I was tired and deflated. On the drive back I called in at a friend's party, passed up a drink, and clambered back into the transit van I'd borrowed, ready for home, a bath, and bed. By this time I was feeling easier about the day, so I drove slowly across the Menai Bridge, enjoying the evening sky, subdued but calm.

The stretch of road from Menai Bridge to Beaumaris traces a path along the coast and was known locally to us as Millionaire's Row. The road makes extravagant curves, twisting in on itself as it flexes to the geology of the hillside. The trees are mature beeches and oaks, and large expensive houses crouch behind evergreen shrubberies and fences that ask the world to keep its distance. I swung the transit into the first of the curves and saw the speedometer nuzzle forty miles per hour.

Looking back now I wonder at the space of time that becomes sandwiched between life as normal and the sudden impact of colossal, irrevocable change. I imagine that time suddenly becomes compressed, almost shrinking back from the demand of the new challenge. An in-breath, an almost imperceptible hesitation. I had a brief view of a car tilting round the corner ahead. It was way over on my side of the road and travelling very fast. Headlights flared and I felt the shock of realisation that comes when you know you have met the unavoidable, and that pain is on its way to visit you. My world became dark, shot through with red flashes and a terrible shrieking noise. Everything loosened, became detached and unfamiliar. I felt a tearing, screaming jolt, and heard myself crying out words I cannot now remember. The windscreen imploded and I was flung against the steering wheel, twisted and shaken like a mouse in the jaws of its killer. Then it was still. I think I was only unconscious for a few seconds. As I opened my eyes I saw and I knew that it was bad. Very bad. I was choking and coughing, and fumbling to feel myself, trying to sense the extent of my injuries, terrified that I would find a limb missing. Blood was spilling down my face and I felt as if I'd been hammered and pulverised for hours. The door wouldn't open but I managed to clamber out of the cabin through the gaping hole where the windscreen had been. Steam was pouring from engines, twisted metal lay wrenched and torn. The other car, a Mini, was just a few feet ahead and violently concertina-ed. Hundreds of unrelated and confused thoughts jostled in my mind – the fear of explosions, the other driver, the smell of petrol, the taste of blood, and the need for help. I was stumbling, falling, getting up again, and staring wildly around. Groping my way round the wreckage I stared into the cab of the other car. I had never seen a dead person before. A shock of massive proportions shook me. I think I was trying to speak. Head uplifted, mouth open, saliva and blood, the body was completely caged in a metallic rictus of anger and hate. I think I was sobbing.

I forget the next few minutes but I found myself fighting my way through a shrubbery, trying to find help. I couldn't seem to locate a path or drive so I was flailing my way through bushes hoping that I would come soon to a house. More time passed and I recall lying on gravel in front of a large imposing house. Lurching upwards I stumbled to the door and leaned against the doorbell. I could hear it sounding in the hall and heard doors opening. Then silence. Again I pressed the bell, this time calling out for help, occasionally falling down. A window opened above me and I tottered backwards trying to look up.

'There's been an accident. Please call for the police.....and an ambulance. Please hurry.' I fell down again, disorientated and feeling very alone. The faces above me peered down, frightened, condemning.

'Go away. We can't help you.'

I tried again 'Please, you don't understand. There's been an accident ...'

'Go away. We don't know who you are. We'll call the police ...'

'Yes, yes. I don't want anything ... just please do ... please do call ...'

I fell consumed with despair. I imagined that the young woman in the car might still somehow be alive. I could not believe, and I still can't, that these people allowed their own fear to rampage so mercilessly in their minds as to preclude performing even the simplest act of compassion. I remember turning away, then darkness, until I became aware of my head cradled in someone's lap. They were comforting me. It was a man. Apparently he had driven by the accident and found me unconscious, sprawled on the pavement, by the cars. He called the emergency services. The police arrived first. Up until this time I had had a somewhat jaundiced view of the police. It changed that night. I remember marvelling at the kindness I was shown, the care, and the gentle strength that made me comfortable. Words of reassurance were spoken and for the first time in what seemed like hours I felt safe.

A month later I went back to the scene of the accident. I wanted to find the house that had figured so poignantly in my nightmare. I wanted to find those people and tell them how much I despised them: their pathetic little castle, their pathetic little compromised lives, but I couldn't find it. I even tried again some weeks later, but everything seemed different, and the need and the time passed. Now, twenty years later, I still occasionally think on that time and the challenge that suddenly thrust itself upon those people's lives. Perhaps they were kind after all. Perhaps some fantasy of fear momentarily engulfed their good intentions. Perhaps later on they had to spend some hours trying to talk their way into excusing their meanness, their fear. Life visits us with experiences that test who we are, and the shining mirror is held up once more so that we can see who we really are. Surprised, caught off balance, it would be very easy to disappoint ourselves.

Sometimes it seems that death is a bit like this. We spend all our lives somehow believing that we will always live, that the being who stares out on life from behind these eyes must be immortal. We imagine that we have so much time. So much time that we can afford to fill it with all kinds of things that bring us no joy, give nothing to anybody else, and weaken our ability to be the person we once dreamed of being. We just fill space and get old. The woman that died in the Mini that night had had an argument in a pub in Beaumaris. It was an argument between lovers. At the inquest it was implied that she may have driven her car at mine deliberately. I found that very hard. I found it hard to accept that someone might have chosen me to kill themselves against, and while I suppose it shouldn't make any difference, it felt all the harder for it being a woman. Now I carry a few scars to remind me of the time. They are not so easy to see. When I had recovered I began to create a garden, and that garden has gone on growing inside me ever since. I will never leave it. I will never betray the chance I was given to reconsider what I think of as being important. I shall burn my fire as bright as I can. This way I shall see the Invisible Path and I will set my heart to following it.

The real terror of dying is the knowledge of a life wasted, of the gifts that have been heaped upon us cast up and thrown away, of opportunities sacred as the earth herself left on a forgotten sidewalk, bereft for want of courage.

Once I was recovered I began a task that was as big symbolically as it was in effort. Some months before I had arrived with a group of friends outside the doors of a place called Limestone Manor. We were looking for somewhere to hold one of the first One Earth Gatherings, and the omens were good. I took a walk around the grounds and found myself in a very beautiful south-facing, two-tiered Victorian walled garden. Nothing grew in this garden except lawns of grass and two types of Valerian on the walls. A dovecote stood at the southern end by a wrought iron gate, and there was a gardener's bothy in the west. At this time in my life, having tried my hand at many things, my friend Nick and I were now coming to the end of a one-year training as gardeners at Plas Newydd estate on Mona.

As I stood looking at this garden it seemed to me that I was invited to bring it back to life. I imagined a garden that would speak to people about spirit while also providing the manor kitchen with vegetables. It seemed to me that spirit and food and shelter, and all the basics of life, should exist side by side supporting each other and telling the same tale. Limestone Manor was a management training centre and one of many similar centres opening at the time. It offered courses in leadership, team building and personal development. However, Limestone was also unique, and not least because Gary was the proprietor. It was 1982 and Gary had emerged from the corporate world with a good idea. He was a character of almost indefatigable energy and immense reservoirs of self-belief. He was creative, resourceful, charismatic, and very charming. He also had one or two blind spots, and a tendency never to believe anything that sounded like bad news unless it was himself saying it, which he never did. He was big-hearted, generous and visionary. I had told him what I'd like to do with the walled garden and he'd given me the keys.

Now, battered, bruised, and deeply introspective, I began to mark out the beds

Mac gardening at Limestone Manor

and lift the turf. I had in mind a design based upon the Native American Medicine Wheels, of which I had a hazy and incomplete understanding. Looking back, it would be like someone saying they spoke French because they could recite the verb 'to be'. Nevertheless, together with Nick and some other close friends, we knew we were on to something, and the garden was my intuitive response. Into the garden I brought a tipi, erected it, and moved in. The training at Plas Newydd estate, the car accident, and the garden at Limestone Manor somehow all conspired together to bring me to a place of far deeper commitment. Two decisions were made during this time that set both my course and Nick's for years to come. We began working with business executives and we began to search for a path that would take us deeper into spirit. A third decision had already been taken, an understanding that we had somehow to come closer to the real things that spoke to us spiritually: earth, flowers, freedom. Neither of us was in the first flush of youth. We were in our mid-thirties, pretty much adrift, knowing that there was work to be done but unsure where and how. When I think of that time I see myself on the hillside of my dream, binoculars scanning the horizon as I anxiously search for the Invisible Path, and all the time it glows and pulses by my feet.

It took a journey of some 4,000 miles to find someone who could slap me hard enough before I would sit up and take notice.

Isle of Erraid Journal – 3

Many of the consulting assignments that I have undertaken involve an individual or a team that in one way or another needs to embrace change and adapt. As I research the situation and formulate my strategy I look for the imperatives. It is so much easier to facilitate change if the people involved can see and understand why it is necessary to change, why they should endure the discomfort. There may yet be a need to express anger and mourn what is passing before uncertainly glancing to the new horizon, but understanding the imperatives helps.

In 2004 for the first time in my life I visited one of the South African townships outside Johannesburg. In the same year I travelled to India and walked the streets of Mumbai's slum districts, met with dedicated people working in the field for Action Aid and the World Wildlife Fund, and witnessed the crushing poverty of Mozambique's indomitable rural population. Everywhere there are imperatives as large as life itself, and all demand change. However, when I review my own personal response to the anguish and despair that human ignorance and greed has bestowed upon the world, I have a different realisation. It goes deeper. The power that will bring us to change is love. In the privileged backwaters of suburban Britain we will not choose to accept greater inconvenience in our lives on the basis of fear, but because we care. Beauty is as essential to our well-being as food and water. Of course, if we don't allow ourselves to become vulnerable in this way, then eventually compulsion will fill the need, and change will be visited upon us whether we co-operate or not.

It's not a question of whether another 100 or 200 or 300 animal and plant species die in the next day or two, and whether or not this is relevant to the survival of human beings. What matters to me is that they are now extinct, and that in earlier years my indifference contributed to this irreversible loss. It matters to me that we have logged out most of the great forests of our world, whether or not we can make do with what's left. It matters to me that the cod no longer exist in the Grand Banks and are now under severe threat in the North Atlantic, whether or not we can live without cod. It matters to me that the fishermen no longer have jobs and that the fishing fleet is now rotting in harbour, when both cod and fishermen could have prospered. It matters to me that the air we breathe should be so polluted, even if we can manufacture inhalers which keep us from choking.

I think of the Earth in the same way that I think about my garden. I care for my garden. I have a responsibility to it, and this includes all the living beings with whom I share it. I work to see it pulse with life, sound, scent, colour, food, everything. I need to protect my garden. This way of thinking, this way of feeling, brings me great joy. It allows me to walk on my land with some sense of pride and humility. The moment that this becomes our way of being with our gardens, the door opens to a realisation that the Earth is our garden, and to the garden we have a duty.

CHAPTER THREE

Venturing abroad

Until I was able to find my way through the layers of misinformation and conformity that obfuscated my perception of society's cultural mores I had to make do with what I was told. Obliquely, insidiously, yet no less powerful for that, we are told who we are from the youngest age. Unless we're fortunate enough to have the benefit of wiser counsel, most of what we're told has very little to do with anything of any significance or real meaning. Once noticed, this thought leads us on to the logical conclusion that life is not of any real significance – a kind of feeble fluttering that goes unnoticed until it crumples and gives up. For instance, in our culture we're given names that at least thousands of others living already have, and millions of dead have had before that. These names mean nothing to us personally. It may be that some had meaning once, but in general they are picked out of a hat because our parents like the sound of them, and for reasons that have more to do with them than us. On one occasion I had a group of five managers in my care on an open leadership programme. Every one had the name Dave. They even looked similar. It led to moments of real confusion and great hilarity, but in the end we solved it by creating names that reflected something unique and special about each person. The naming of each manager by the others in the group became a way of celebrating who they really were. They wore their names with pride. That is until they turned to meet the outside world; then they became embarrassed, and carefully, regretfully, left them behind.

Then we are informed of the expectations that our family has of us. This is still very little to do with us, most especially since what is expected is that we 'fit in' and conform to the unspoken and spoken rules that govern our particular circumstances. Unless we do it for ourselves we remain externally defined and our sense of identity can never be anything other than counterfeit and necessarily frail. Youth must shake the elder's staff. They must be given the chance to renew the society they have been born to, given the chance to laser through our complacent traditions and find out who they truly are. This way we get a second chance, and it is also why it's so important that we keep in touch with the young. Of course youth itself is insecure and often immensely susceptible to peer pressure and externally imposed icons that purport to represent them. We have entire industries dedicated to this right now, and they have us by the throat. When you think about it, it's incredible that corporations should have successfully persuaded us that without their logo on our shirt we are somehow to be excluded. We are afraid of becoming a non-person so we wear the logo, and paradoxically we are lost in our fear-driven need to belong. It's not just the young who have succumbed to this either.

I was very fortunate to have parents who generally supported the view that we should make our own discoveries and do our own thinking. Conversation was encouraged and mealtimes were often noisy with debate, but I became increasingly aware of the stifling conformity that adult life held as the great prize and reward for enduring a good education. In fact enduring extremes of hypocrisy, although very painful, are useful when we're trying to unravel this stuff.

There is no human power more precious than imagination. As a species we have deployed our imagination across the full spectrum of possibility; from the numinous to the sickeningly brutal. It is human imagination that produced the poetry of Blake, the ancient artistry of the cave paintings, the passion and conviction that impelled Mary Wollstonecraft to dedicate her life to freedom, equality and democracy. Imagination takes us to the heart of creation. If we ever track imagination to its source, we will find pure spirit and the wellspring of all the worlds.

Yet imagination is a power and it does not restrict itself to the poet or the artist. It is available to us all, including the crass and dangerous in equal measure. We have only to consider any of the wars that have filled our newspapers over recent years to meet human imagination at work. We can see other expressions of human imagination in much of the food that we eat, in our mania to possess, our disregard for beauty, and our willingness to throw our lives to the cold caress of institutions that serve only abstract inhuman values. It is human imagination that unscrupulous proselytisers of a corrupted religion used to fuel the burning of countless women, children, and men across western Europe from the 12th to the 18th century. Yet imagination remains a gift of unparalleled value for its capacity to birth beauty. It enables us as human beings to reach into places that exist at the periphery of possibility, in pure and applied science, in art and in spirit.

Imagination is the beginning of everything. It thrives on diversity in all its forms, it loves new experience, and it needs constant renewal. We need stimulation to mind, emotions, body and spirit, for imagination to soar and return from the skies with the gifts of Helios, of healing. Imagination is a close companion to play, and we need play because it lifts us up and energises us, so that all that is familiar becomes new again. Play is not only for children. It is not only children who learn from play – adults need it also, but not the organised synthetic play that requires no effort. Children work hard at play. Like everything else, you get back what you put in. I have been taught that children learn by building structures – conceptually, psychologically, physically, emotionally; they perceive the world and create structures through which to interpret experience. For adults to learn they have to apply the opposite process and undo many of the structures that now imprison their perception and limit their thinking. What served us well in the early years now obscures reality. Beliefs, prejudices, attitudes – all serve to hold life at arm's length.

But the imagination that I'm speaking of is not something in which we can be trained. It is not available to anybody unless they are still dreaming, still open to the possibility of radical change. If I organise my life on the basis that I can only ever get richer, never poorer, then what will this do to my imagination? It stops you dead in your tracks, spiritually at least. Risk becomes something to avoid at all costs. For a great many it also means that they can never actually get rich. Imagination lives for the adventures that will set the world alight, and this never exists without risk and challenge.

Twenty years ago I successfully employed my imagination to great effect and made some changes.

I remembered the small boy who could create whatever he wanted simply by exerting his imagination. The small boy who only needed some earth and grass and could then travel anywhere in this world or any other. A few metres of derelict wasteland would have served the same purpose. I remembered a power that has graced me on more than a few occasions over the years, and I deployed it again.

'Dying is easy, it's living that scares me.' – Annie Lennox

So when, after many faltering steps, stumbles, bruises and some sadness, I suddenly found the door hidden in the wardrobe, and found it unlocked, I didn't wait for a beckoning. I jumped.

During the flight from Heathrow to San Francisco I had the first intimation of flu. I could feel the tickling in my throat and my temperature was soaring. By the time the plane landed I was feeling rough, and by the time I made it into the coach and was travelling north towards Nevada City I was feeling profoundly ill. I already knew that I was walking into one of the most important and confrontational episodes of my life. After several years of searching, Nick and I had found some people who seemed to have the knowledge and depth we had been hunting for. It rapidly becomes apparent to anyone who has made the journey that there is no other pathway more fraught with tricksters, fools, inadequate, sex-obsessed, money-obsessed, power-obsessed, egotistical charlatans than the spiritual path. What makes it even more dangerous is that many actually believe that they are what they say they are, and, as if this wasn't difficult enough, everybody you used to count as friends thinks you're an idiot and should return to the fold. We had been to see different people and we had done our reading, but most of all, thankfully, we had pursued our own direct experience and we had made some startling discoveries. We already knew that spirit was reality and that neither of us could live without knowing that our lives made sense in this context. We had glimpsed the Invisible Path and we were dedicated to following wherever it took us. Nick was coming in on a later flight and would arrive a few days later. Until then I was on my own; so, shivering, my nose a cataract of catarrh and mucus, I gingerly stepped down from the bus and stood with my bags looking around. A stolid, swarthy, slightly threatening individual detached himself from the shadows of a pseudo-colonial shop front and flowed across the road towards me.

'Hi', I said brightly.

He didn't speak but took my proffered hand and gave it a perfunctory disinterested squeeze. Taking my smaller bag he turned his back on me and walked towards a pick-up parked a little way off on the other side of the street. Grabbing hold of my rucksack I took my cue and adopted a rather less friendly, more surly demeanour.

'Far to go ...?'

'Not far.'

I nodded, burying my head in a paper tissue and exploding it with another appalling sneeze.

'Not feeling so good ...' I admitted, and immediately regretted this admission of weakness. I sensed I was losing ground fast.

'What's your name?' This time I'd dropped my voice an octave, and had adopted an expression of what I hoped might be interpreted as lazy indifference.

'Eyes of the night.'

'What ...?'

'Eyes of the night.'

I paused. This was hopeless.

'What's yours?'

'Tim.'

We made the rest of the journey in silence but I sensed that he was feeling very satisfied with our first encounter. As for me, I was struggling to maintain some sense of personal authority. Eyes of the Night was not the person I'd come to see. Whoever lay at the other end of this car journey was a good deal more powerful than my driver, but right now I was seriously wondering if I had the resources to cope with what lay ahead. 'Coping' is a very English word. That's what we often do, cope. I hated the idea of 'coping'. I wasn't coping very well. I resolved to stop coping and stand up a little straighter. Then I sneezed again.

Eventually, deep in the forest, the car pulled to a standstill and I fell out of the pick-up. A short while later I was standing by the tipi where I was to be accommodated over the coming weeks, and taking in my surroundings. Even with my health in free fall I still caught my breath as I took in my surroundings and allowed the enormity of my situation to settle on my awareness. I had tried to be a good Christian, I had explored meditation and I'd washed myself in the *Bhagavad Gita* and the *Upanishads*. Eventually, I had stood by a blazing fire on a beach somewhere in Wales and accepted that wind, rain, earth, fire, trees, women, delicious food, snow, fresh coffee, the scent of flowers, steaming horse dung, mist, frost, the hearth of friends, sailing boats, and the moon – these were my loves. These were my passions, these were everything that made life worth living, and I had to find a way of walking with my own loves, not the trodden path of belief, but a way that sang to my heart in the wild cadences of the sun herself.

I watched as he made his way towards me. A big man, kind of scary looking, relaxed, but electricity fizzing from every edge. He felt dangerous.

'What's your name?' The voice was direct, compelling, requiring an answer.

'Bad start', I thought, and then aloud, 'Tim'.

'Tim who?'

'Macartney'.

'Ah ...'

So far so good. I risked another sneeze. Eyes from beneath the rim of a cowboy hat drilled into me before passing above my head and moving to the far distance.

'Do you know what it means?'

'What?'

'Macartney.' A touch of irritation.

'Yes, I think it means Son of Arthur.'

'Good, yes... the Son of Arthur... !'

The voice filled the forest. It swept me up and dropped me on the floor. It wasn't just the volume, it was the resonance the words had with my own longing.

'Mac Arthur, a proud name... ! So, what does Arthur mean?'

The momentum of our interaction was increasing with every second. I felt as if I was swinging towards a cliff edge. No reply formed itself on my lips and he cut in again shifting through layers of old English, Norse, and German.

'...Ar-Thur, Thur, Thor, THOR! You are the son of THOR! BE... THAT... MAN !!'

Silence, and I could hear the cold. I was sick with longing, sick with firing on three cylinders, sick of being anything less than Thor's son. I was a son of this magnificent earth. I had known who I was all my life but I had never allowed myself to 'be that man'.

The voice sliced the evening air again.

'The earth is alive.'

'Yes, yes, I know it is...'

'No, you don't get it. The Earth is Alive.'

'Yes. The earth is alive.'

'NO!... listen you dumbfuck, THE EARTH... IS... ALIVE!!'

And again the silence. My mind rang and rang, the Earth is Alive, and he left, walking up the way he'd come.

The trapdoor is eased into position and then thuds closed, and the darkness is complete. My two companions are in here with me, but they might as well be on the other side of the world. Earth and rock all around. For some this would feel like a tomb, yet the words tomb and womb have the same root and I choose the latter. I am familiar with this place.

The worlds shift, gyrate, fade and focus. I find a better position, relaxing, letting my breathing slow. There are experiences that we know are just waiting to happen – this, for me, was one such. For ten days, with occasional times above ground, the Kiva holds us in darkness; darkness so profound, so absolute, so holding of possibility. I journey between the planets. I no longer have a sense of limits or containment. How paradoxical that, in this small underground ceremonial chamber, with the trapdoor firmly closed, and light only a memory, I should feel so free and sense only the huge vastness of unlimited, eternal space and time. What will be born in this place of dreaming?

In the sacred space of the Kiva, dreaming with the Earth, I contemplate my experience. How true am I to the experience that life gives me?

And then... what – do – I – see... ?

I see light. My mind balks, resistant to the information it is receiving. Yet, undeniably, light is present. All is dark. Yet, I see light ... billions of particles of light, colours, all swirl and dance, happy for my recognition. In the darkest place there is light. Yet does the presence of light somehow make darkness okay? Is darkness not beautiful and sacred as darkness? What is this I see squirming in my mind? Is it a belief? Who put it there? Darkness holds in protection so much that otherwise would die. The animals do not judge the dark. If there are predators out there in the darkness it is the torch beam that will betray me, not the refuge of blackened night. A sudden dive, a deepening – from the dark is born another thought. In the most brilliant light there exists darkness. Is this not what the poets have spoken of – the dark sun?

Days and nights pass, with all the edges lost in the deep, timeless turning of a mind that leaps upon imagination's steed and travels countless millions of miles. A wrenching sound and the light of evening floods the buried chamber. We have visitors. Down into this lair of dreams comes a drum. A big drum, delicately decorated: the Mother drum. Alert, taut, eyes narrowed, listening, waiting; aware of the moon as her deep magic bathes the Kiva before the door closes once more. The drum talks, insistent, direct – a huge sound filling the void of space. The singers send out a song, and I find the wilderness in my heart. I am up. I dance. I add my voice, and the sound reverberates against the looming walls, picking me up and hurling me out into deep space.

It is the ninth night. Up until this day I had been vegetarian for fifteen years. Sitting in the Kiva, journeying the Invisible Path, now listening to the drum that beats in the heart of our Earth. Knowing that the sun lives on in the centre of the Earth, still pulsing. Voyaging distant lands, coming to a place of knowing not previously encountered, remembering and remembering; perceiving the wheel of all things living and glimpsing essence. I turn and walk another way. The healer and the killer walk out from the Kiva and take the proffered blade. There is no avoiding the death that gives me life. Without anger, without pleasure, swiftly and in appreciation, the life is yielded that I can eat and have life. It is the ninth night and the Kiva door shuts once more. Light is gone. Only the quietness and the breath.

I start with shock. A sharp intake of breath. As clear as any TV screen a picture forms, suspended in the darkness. The goose, whose life was taken under the blade I held, lies on the ground, its head now separated from the body, dead. Another small sound rises from inside me, I am transfixed. Even as I watch, eyes drilling into the scene before me, a grey-misted shape emerges and detaches from the still corpse, gracefully, effortlessly, a form perfect and complete: a goose. The head and body remain, lifeless and unmoving, as the goose being spreads her broad wings and motions them into flight. She is leaving. Her work is done. Never to leave me, this gift of the Kiva. With the vision comes the knowing of what it is to be blessed.

I see a man who is lost, and yet who is unwilling to entertain the fact that he may have invested years in hiding from himself. A man who desires to grow old before life intended. A man so pained with himself that, before the hammer fell, he walked like one already defeated.

It was once suggested to me that I was so shrouded in sadness that unless I learnt to love the battle, I would never be able to experience life in any way other than fearfully – always secretly trying to avoid it, turning the other way, hoping that it might just pass me by. It was good advice for me, and I've had to fight for every inch to find this place of loving. Now I know that the battlefield is where I belong, and I hope to die there. You and I are made in different ways, but I think that this advice is for you also. The key word in it is 'love', not 'put up with' or 'cope' or 'sort of love'. It is just 'love'. Now that's hard I think, but it could also be wondrous. The thing is we have so little time. Living, dying, it doesn't matter that much; it's 'how' we live. Face your fears, joyfully, leap at them. They were given to you to learn by. I don't think that running away will offer you any kind of peace. I think life will follow wherever you go and bring you challenge. She wants to see if you are the fighter she hopes and prays you are. Get involved – get involved in a way that you never have before. Amaze yourself. Our world does not need another hanger-on, she needs strong women and men who will love her in practical ways. She doesn't ask for physical strength. She asks for spiritual strength, strength of the Spirit. You can be on a stretcher and still be a force to be reckoned with. Once our land was covered in forest. Not any more. She was trashed. Who will fight to see the trees return? Not 'lend a hand', fight to see the trees return. Not you, you think? Why? You think I'm talking to myself? I don't think so. I'm talking about healing, about healing. I understand that you have suffered, and many of those scars you will carry to your grave, but you're in good company because many of us out here also carry similar wounds – some of them savagely inflicted. Introspection has you by the throat. You have some years left. That's all any of us have. How many, is hidden from us. What will you do? I suspect that until you devote your full energies to a cause that is practical, tangible, measurable and passionate, you will not find the place you long for. You have such welts of anger lodged in your gut that if it is not expressed in a positive, active, energetic way, then I fear it will continue to fry you. Sadness kills.

Your friend

Mac

Not altogether surprisingly this letter provoked a furious response. It was written at a time when all manner of dissembling was impossible. In the language of person-centred counselling, I had not been 'congruent'. This letter was an attempt to set this right. It was a canon salvo, and I hoped that while I might lose a friend for a while, I might also stimulate some determination to take up the reins and step away from an overwhelmingly sorrowful, passive and burdened negativity. I still don't know whether the salvo found its mark. More importantly, now some year or so later, I see how my own landscape has shifted. Events and revelations of the past year have seen the internal geological plates of my perception and understanding tilt and change. For many years assumptions that provided me with paving-stones have held inviolate the analogy of the battlefield. This is changing. I continue to perceive life as challenge, but the nature of that challenge admits as many possibilities and potentials as the sphere itself. Turning away from the battlefield, simply turning my steps in another direction, allowing the sword to fall from nerveless fingers – this too can be a challenge. I have fought in many battles, and truthfully, I have something of the soldier in me. When the storm clears and the wind subsides, it is easy to find that your back remains stooped, fists still clenched. It is a challenge to stand upright and acknowledge the invitation to peace. Fists balled into hammers do not easily accept the joy of rest. Striving does not easily yield to flowing.

Isle of Erraid Journal — 4

8.30 a.m. Gazing out of the window in front of my desk, and Bruch accompanies billowing clouds as they heave across the eastern skyline shot through with pinks and a tangerine fringing to their frayed edges. The moon blesses Pier Cottage each evening as she rises in the east and traverses the black northern sky. I think of her as a sentinel, standing guard, and in some way feel protected by her vigilance. Earlier as I woke and pulled back the shutters on my bedroom window I saw her again, now in the west, fading, her task for these isles complete for now. Outside my window is a small paddock in which Erraid's cow and two calves are currently pastured, One of the calves is just two weeks old being born one day before I arrived at Pier Cottage. Each day I've had the pleasure of watching this little family circle and the intimate pleasures and irritations that bring us so close. I never realised how much calves play. Throughout each day she explores, pretends, invents, and provokes. Rushing about madly, getting in the way of the other two, obsessively interested in a metal post that's driven into the ground just twenty feet from my window, she addresses it, teases it and appears to invest it with different personalities. Her sister, now a year old, behaves like any other teenager and intermittently becomes overly serious and self-important, or loses all inhibition and torments her younger sister by interrupting her games and harassing her with irrelevant self-conscious games that don't quite work. The cow remains impassive to all of this except when the older sister becomes a little too boisterous; then she promptly breaks off grazing to step between the two. I've come to realise how well she manages to divide

Sunset from Erraid

her attention between her own needs and the calves' well-being. One thing has struck me deeply which is how busy they are all day. I had the impression that not much goes on for a cow during the day but these three have almost more than they can fit into the daylight hours.

I glance up at the clouds. The pinks have gone and been replaced with blue charcoal greys and the oily cream of sheep's wool. As with yesterday the electricity has shut off again and I'm congratulating myself on bringing the battery power pack. Bruch continues and the computer powers on as I start my ninth day on Erraid. I feel good but delicate. The hours shift me through different emotions as I struggle and dance, flow and judder my way through this task and joy of writing.

The experience of the garden at Limestone for me was seminal. It marked a point of no return. The car accident, and a sense of now or never, persuaded me to focus. For a few years I devoted myself to the task of creating a garden that in principle was like one of those ubiquitous dream-catchers that we see everywhere now. A place that people might stumble across, pause, feel touched, and in some way enriched. In design it was very simple – an oval with four rotating quarters: two paths that ran east-west and north-south, and another that followed the circumference. The garden was located on a south-facing slope and the tipi was placed in the north on a small dais of levelled turf. I was making wooden sculptures at the time and two of these were placed in the garden, along with a forked pole that was planted in the south-west. There was, and is, something special about this garden, hillside and peninsula – a subtlety, and a sense that the rocks are not as solid as you might expect. I felt the land speak to me and I responded, doing all I could to amplify her voice. I was also intent on making my first attempt to speak to a wider audience on issues close to my heart, and somehow this happened. Radio 4, HTV, BBC2, *The Mail on Sunday*, all came and did a piece on this garden. Tourists popped in and I spent an increasing amount of time talking to visitors, or entertaining business managers by the fire in the tipi. Somewhere inside me I became uncomfortable with myself. It didn't feel quite real. Two events occurred over the space of a few months that caused me to hand the garden on to a friend. The first was waking one morning to find two tourists inside the tipi as I lay in bed, seemingly unconcerned that this was my home and chatting to each other while they gave me a cheery 'Good morning'. The second was returning to Limestone to find that a storm had severely damaged the tipi. This was my fault. I had allowed grass to grow up around the tipi base, which in our climate meant that it was perpetually damp. The hem rotted and when the storm came it began to tear. Once started it just got worse. I realised that I needed to focus more on my own journey and learning if I wished to inhabit a more public forum with authenticity. At the same time I was beginning to realise that I had a gift for working with people, that business managers were people, and that I enjoyed their company.

Limestone Manor made use of a number of outdoor management tasks which were designed to provide their corporate clients with the framework for a profound learning experience. They worked very well. Several of those who first gathered to make up the core team at Limestone had created these tasks in such a way that as a facilitator you could shift the emphasis and interpretation of the experience according to the objectives of the programme. Each of these tasks required the managers to absorb information, interpret and analyse, develop strategies, plan resources, apply monitoring systems, and arrange roles within the group. A small number of simple theoretical models were used, with the main emphasis of the learning being placed upon the facilitator's skill in using the events of the day to assist the group in finding transferable learning. For most of us engaged in delivering these courses it was extremely rewarding, confronting, and absorbing work. Business managers poured through Limestone in those days. We would welcome a new group on a Sunday and wave them off the following Saturday. It was exhausting and we loved it.

Accompanying and coaching so many teams of business leaders, I had the opportunity to study leadership and leaders in a way that my unorthodox 'career path' had never made available. Particularly interesting to me was the territory that exists in the no-man's-land between going forward and turning back. A dear friend of mine once asked me how I would define failure. I don't recall my reply, but his definition was 'giving up'. I have found this idea extremely useful. If we are to place ourselves at the edge of our learning, then from time to time we will necessarily confront the crushing finality of impending failure. If then we give up, we are lost – for a time at least. This is not the same as knowing when to change strategy, or even redefine our goals. Sometimes these things are necessary.

Giving up is failure indeed.

Although I have stood in front of disappointment many times, become lazy, fooled and deluded myself, and procrastinated, I have never yet entertained the idea of giving up. The price is too heavy. The Invisible Path has always flickered and pulsed in the half-gloom, patient, waiting. The business leaders I met at Limestone Manor were often impressive both for their fortitude and their skills, but their leadership was ultimately sabotaged by the weakness inherent in the business leader's proposition – a request for dedication – sabotaged by the vapid frailty of maximising shareholder value as the ultimate goal. Who, except perhaps the shareholders themselves, will call upon their deepest reserves and pay such a dear and debilitating price? Fortunately very few. Set against this, however, are the millions who nevertheless submit to a servitude that ultimately doesn't benefit them at all. They may not give their all but nonetheless they give more than anyone should for something of such limited intrinsic value. True leadership needs the presence of something bigger than filling someone else's pockets – or even one's own pockets come to that. To compensate, business leaders have to resort to aliases. In this context an alias is a screen of carrots, sticks, visions and values that serves to obscure the desolate truth and substitute something, anything, that will inspire and motivate. Life requires no alias.

The same passive, hideously powerful lie sits deeply embedded in our Western culture, and we export it everywhere. It does not make us happy. It makes us comfortable. And from then on it's just one more layer of fat. Our lives are controlled by what we cannot see. What is unreal is held aloft as a banner and we flock to participate. Any lie invested with such energy assumes the power of the divine, and it is in this way that we make our obeisance. Self-betrayal on this level takes some commitment, but then we are human, and this is the work of our species. It is the Invisible Path, and the searching for ourselves. With all our ignorance and enormous energy, right now we are creating the circumstances necessary to hasten our transforming consciousness, and when the time comes we will find wisdom.

Seeking a vision is important. I don't recollect my school education informing me that life would be fraught with challenging experience, and that I would do well to gain some clarity as to its meaning and purpose. It was inferred that I should try to get a good job and be happy. It wasn't that helpful. I had a life to lead, and if this was all that was on offer, then I would reject it, break laws, and set myself apart, hurting, but at least with my pride still intact. Some accept what's on offer and only later wake up to find the promise wanting. Some grow sad and get old. Some get angry. All have the resources to find their way, if doing so becomes important enough. Finding work that holds meaning for us is important to our health, particularly as we grow older. I had found part of that meaning, and I was exultant. To be amongst the mountains of Snowdonia in sunshine and storms, walking trails redolent of my imaginal world, exploring leadership with fellow travellers, and searching moments of illumination – I took my apprenticeship seriously.

It takes time and it takes effort. Little by little, piece by piece, we can detect and identify the unconscious patterns that exist behind the weave of choices and compulsions that direct our steps. We imagine that our circumstances are largely determined by luck or, more confidently, choice, but it's more fundamental than that. Synchronicity has depths we'd mostly rather ignore. A pattern of mine that became obvious, and for some years inexplicable, was my unerring gravitation towards harsh and intimidating experiences that took me deep inside unsafe territory.

Over many occasions now I have found myself in the company of people who in some way or other walk a dangerous, painful and dark-shadowed world. I made strenuous efforts to distance myself from this subterranean Plutonic landscape, but I had appointments to keep and life obliged. I was so convinced that the decision to walk spiritually meant that all I had to do was be 'good', I never realised the immense process of unravelling that is the walking of the Invisible Path. It has taken some courage to understand that I must meet and make relationship with the interior psychological landscape of the deep forest. Traversing trails that were many times frightening, I have come right up hard against fat welts of sadness, power abused and broken dreams. Sometimes the experience has had a pitiless quality that has removed all humour and joy, but in many cases it has been less harsh. Gary, Limestone Manor's visionary leader, was a case in point. Gary accepted no checks and balances. He was 'right'. Very talented and often charismatic, self-doubt never seemed to penetrate his world. Only deep beneath the waves was there something more honest, nestling, awaiting the kiss of a faerie prince. Affectionate, warm, beguiling and manipulative, he probably still believes that he was somehow the heroic victim of a gross injustice.

I learned a lot from Gary.

When Limestone Manor eventually collapsed we discovered that Gary's delusional world had cost us heavily. Bad debts abounded, pension funds plundered, angry revengeful thoughts – Gary's exit was not graceful. The wronged became looters, and soon there was nothing left, except the shell of a big house, the echoes of past laughter, the garden, and birdsong. The land was not harmed, and the humans moved on searching for new experience.

Looking east from Limestone Manor's garden you can see the mountains.

The gorge was a place in which the symbolism of waterfalls, deep pools, and sheer rock faces could awaken even the most jaded corporate executive. I cannot imagine that any management training centre still exists that uses Dolgarrog Gorge in the way in which it was originally used, and for that we should all be extremely grateful. Nevertheless, while understanding that it infringes all necessary and important safety principles (and laws), I recall with fondness the raw exhilaration that we encountered there and which provided so many with experiences I doubt they will ever forget.

As the name suggests the gorge is a deeply incised river course that slices into an escarpment on the southern edge of the Conway valley in North Wales. It has been, and I expect it still is, used very safely and professionally by many outdoor education centres, but in the early 1980s things weren't quite the same as they became even just a few short years later. If you follow the river to its source you come to a reservoir that has a tipping gate which, when activated by high water levels in the reservoir, will precipitously jettison thousands of tons of water down the gorge. To witness this spectacle while safely lodged high up on the cliff banks was awe-inspiring. To experience it when negotiating some particularly tricky manoeuvre

in the river bed, was certainly exciting, and possibly terminal. There was a proce-
dure that we used to employ to ascertain whether the gorge was safe or not, and in
the early days this amounted to a gut decision on whether it had been raining much
in the last few days. A while later it used to involve a call to the Central Electricity Gen-
erating Board who monitored water levels in the reservoir, and later still it necessi-
tated a visit to the reservoir to establish visibly the safety or otherwise of the
conditions. I began using the gorge during the first phase and then continued to do
so over the period that a fail-safe system was put in place and used.

Leadership and teambuilding were the two most common areas of focus when we
used the gorge task. The task itself had a number of variations but most were built
around following a prescribed route, indicated on a hand-drawn map, and negotiating the hazards on the way. It worked very well and all kinds of drama took place
within this confined, noisy, and very beautiful corner of the Conway valley. The largest
and most formidable waterfall was known as Waterfall 4. In itself, and as a climbing
route, it was nothing very special for most reasonably fit executives, providing they
didn't suffer from vertigo. When the tipping gate was activated, Waterfall 4 was transformed into something that wouldn't have looked out-of-place in equatorial Africa.
Huge volumes of water thundered over the falls crashing on the rocks below. The
noise was deafening and in appearance it was quite shocking – especially if you
believed that you were shortly to be roped up and sent to meet the worst it could give
you.

On one particular occasion I was with Gary. He was energetically applying himself to the reconstruction of the leader's internalised understanding of what leadership was all about. This was causing some consternation in the team, and of course,
with the leader, who resembled a fly hopelessly caught in the web of a very large and
voracious spider. In full flow Gary was a force to be reckoned with. Rounding a corner, and finding it increasingly difficult to hear anything anyone said, we observed
Waterfall 4 in all its magnificence. I was serving my apprenticeship and under strict
instructions to observe Gary's technique while lending a hand with safety (which is
how it was expressed at that time). It was winter and, with the gorge a raging torrent,
we had already been submerged up to our necks on several occasions. I was very
impressed with the theory and practice of experiential learning since I could observe
at first hand that it had a pulverising educative effect on the delegates. Any precon-
ceived ideas about British men being reluctant to show their feelings, even tears,
had been scotched after my first outing, and I was fully committed to learning the
process skills. Unable to communicate, and with Gary leading, we made our way up

Waterfall climbing in the Conway Valley

to a rock enclave where we were able to absorb the full impact of the waterfall while also planning the assault. From a psychological point of view it was an interesting way of approaching immense personal challenge. The noise was impossible to ignore, the challenge ahead was immediately and visibly enormous, the leader was in the very early stages of hypothermia, and his team were clearly lacking in enthusiasm. Add to this a personal coach, Gary, who for all his good intentions, is irritating, confrontational, elusive and very demanding, and the knowledge that even after Waterfall 4 we are still less than half-way up, and it was a remarkably resilient manager who did not experience some loss of composure. It was at this point that Gary would ramp up the emotional charge of the group with the use of a number of well-aimed questions that would usually reveal that the team were hopelessly unprepared, lacking direction, and doomed to failure. Because considerable time had already been taken to explain that what was experienced on these tasks would be a perfect mirror of the situation at work, it didn't take a genius to work out that the future was not bright, in or out of the gorge. In this way the world became momentarily very hostile, dangerous, unfriendly, and unsupportive.

On this occasion the leader had become very quiet, pale, and unresponsive. Gary was bawling in his ear, and I was marvelling at the dedication these people had to self-improvement. I snapped out of my reverie when I heard Gary say that 'it' was safe. It had never crossed my mind that we were actually going to climb the falls since I had already been assured by a more experienced colleague that they avoided the falls when it was in flood. Well, it was in flood, but it seemed that Gary had stated that it was safe and since he was the expert we were going ahead. As a concession to their inexperience he volunteered to go first and set up a safety line, so we watched in silent appalled horror as he swathed himself in harnesses, karabiners, slings, chocks, belay devices, and a long coil of climbing rope. Then turning to face the waterfall he advanced on it like a veteran gladiator. Standing at the base of the waterfall he surveyed the situation and then suddenly plunged out of view as he dived through the wall of water. Minutes passed and I could hardly bring myself to peek a look at the team. Whatever blood had remained flowing in their veins now seemed to have drained to their feet. Immobile, uncomprehending, aghast at the commitment they were about to undertake, we were all transfixed as we gazed at the water. No sign of Gary. I was beginning to fidget as the uncomfortable awareness dawned on me that I might be called to take some kind of action soon. I was steeling myself when there was a collective group gasp as a hand erupted through the wall of water some twelve inches above the place he'd entered ten minutes ago and flailing in mid air, manacled itself to a wedge of rock. Gary had very impressive hands. They were both large and muscular. If Gary's hands couldn't make it ... All eyes watched this hand as it visibly strove to maintain purchase and pull. In that moment I knew, with all my heart, that for a brief moment at least we were a team – praying that he should fail. He didn't give up on the first attempt, but after this first magnificent effort had resulted in failure we somehow knew that he wasn't going to make it. Conversation struck up in the group as we waited for Gary to call it a day and withdraw. When finally he did the group had a plan and Gary was not in a condition to gainsay it, so we moved off and on to the next obstacle.

The ravines and mountain trails of Snowdonia held enormous symbolic importance for me. I understood that the same trails existed within me, in some kind of hidden world, and that it was urgently necessary for me to bring all my worlds together. I loved the physical world, and I also understood that physically walking the high ridges, probing the woodland valleys, and bathing myself in beauty – with each step I came closer to myself, and to the heart of my seeking. I saw how dislocated so many people are from everything that sets their lives in context. How very rarely we ever look beyond our own feet and the silly childishness of pretend lives.

Isle of Erraid Journal – 5

Everything in creation reflects a spiritual truth. Mysteries that will eventually be decoded are written in capitals all around us. If we have learnt that a tree is worthless, a dead thing, an ornament to be manipulated to our purposes, how can it ever be otherwise? If we have already decided that the mountain is dead matter, that water is only valuable if it has a use that we can exploit, then it will always be just that. Dead, or at least dead to us. But what are we if we are not stone or water, air, earth? Where did we come from? Let's remind ourselves that at one time there were no organisms in existence that conventional wisdom would describe as alive. Out of this deadness we came, carried by a long, long line of relatives. And the story is not yet finished. The creatures I encounter on my walks, the mice, hares, seals and birds, they are my relatives - literally, scientifically. Our genes were born from the same star and they are scarcely different. The life of the hare is my life. I am not better than he. Both of us wish to live, and both of us will strive to keep living. If circumstances became extreme I would try to kill the hare for food. He knows this, and so the essence of the hare and others like him, rabbits, deer, tadpoles, grow in numbers that can provide their relatives with food - the owls, the foxes, the badgers. Eventually we are all food for something. Yet I can still have love for him and respect his life and his place upon this earth, and if one day I have to kill him, I will not do it lightly, or for fun. Why should I? He is my brother.

CHAPTER FOUR

Advances and setbacks

The squabbles, the times of injured pride, the harsh silences that couples allow to impregnate their love and then rot its core.

The splintered barbs of hurt feelings and misunderstandings that fly between parents and teenage children.

The flawed judgement of a bruised ego fighting to reassert itself, unwilling to become vulnerable to the possibility of further loss.

The engulfing loneliness of friendships that founder at a parting of ways when we could have hugged and wished them well.

The horror of admitting our sense of inadequacy and the self-confrontation this would imply.

So much of healing and growing concerns risk and our relationship with it.

There is a model used in organisations that skirmishes with this idea. At the centre there is a circle. This circle is our comfort zone. The comfort zone includes everything with which we are familiar – our habitual environment. In this zone we go about our business with confidence, knowing that we are unlikely to be surprised, or that if we are, we can find an appropriate response. The comfort zone is important. Usually, but not always, it provides us with a place in which we can feel good about ourselves. It can also describe past achievements if what sits within it has been earned in some way. Beyond the comfort zone we enter the risk zone. Most true learning involves stepping inside the risk zone because it necessitates venturing into the unknown. The risk zone is a place of experimentation and adventure. It is not comfortable. If it is, then we are not where we thought we were. Our relationship with risk has a long history. It traverses our early learning environments together with innate inherited pre-dispositions. At the outer extremity of the risk zone we enter a third zone, panic. The panic zone is extreme. Learning is still possible, even profound, but the overall theme is survival and hence failure tends to come with an expensive price tag. We don't usually enter the panic zone voluntarily, and teachers that take us there are rarely teachers for whom integrity counts for much. Working with a group of financial traders from one of the large investment banks, I suggested their place of work was, for most of them, firmly lodged in the comfort zone. This drew a hostile response from the star performer of the group.

'You've got to be kidding. It's never comfortable here!'

Yet it was, of course. He was a duck in water, and proud of it. The same individual became extremely agitated every time the group made tentative steps towards less tangible and more emotive issues. One person's comfort zone can be someone else's recurring nightmare.

You'd think that you'd be safe in the comfort zone. Not so. In the centre of the comfort zone there is an abyss. It works like this.

Nothing in life is static, and, while the universe is still expanding, our comfort zones are forever showing the disconcerting tendency to contract. It's like a muscle. It has to be exercised, and in this area that means visiting the risk zone. A few years away from teenagers, and young people are suddenly alien and a little frightening. Physical challenges that we might have entertained without a second thought when younger assume immense proportions if we have allowed ourselves to become sedentary and prematurely cautious. And of course the same happens with our thinking. If we try to play it safe and stay behind locked doors, we lose touch with what is on the other side. In losing touch we become suspicious and then fearful. What once sufficed as a closed door now requires a sophisticated padlock. Yet we know that no lock exists that can withstand the tenacity of our most feared enemy. So we retreat to the living-room and our world closes in tighter.

A life without risk is a slow, lingering and lonely death.

It's complicated being a human. We may choose another strategy and strive to live forever in the risk zone as the Dice man. But if we are that frightened of the comfort zone, maybe we confused one for the other, in which case ... ?

Some of us are terrified of the responsibility that the material world demands and seek retreat in a kind of pseudo-spirituality. Others fear the world of thinking and deride it in favour of intuition or emotion. Some fear the unpredictable oceans of emotion that surge beneath what is safe, and pour scorn on the less rational. Some draw back from the stars and denounce spirit, trusting only the deposit box safely tucked away in their comfort zone. There have been many others I've encountered who use vast amounts of energy servicing their own internalised struggle, and have never managed to bring their shining talents forward.

From the earliest years we are invited to engage with risk. It is how we learned to walk, to communicate, to relate, to do and to be. Risk is not stepping forward to take. It is opening our arms to life and saying 'welcome'. It is our willingness to love and be loved.

For many years my relationship with risk was highly selective.

1990. It was the end of another year, the second year of my company, Pathways, and we'd been going so hard it felt as if I had never done anything else in my life. Richard, Pathways' only other full-time employee at the time, had left the office and was on his way home. The phone was silent and there was no more to do, for this year at least. I stood by the window and gazed out onto the street, watching the man from the gents' barbers who always stood by his door watching people pass. I looked up to the heavily curtained windows opposite and again speculated on what they might hide. I watched people drift in and out of the Danish Laundry, and once again idly wondered, why Danish? Moving to London had been a good idea. I knew I was there to give Pathways the best possible chance of success, and I was very determined, but there was a cost. I missed the sea, and I missed the mountains. I missed friends, and I missed having a garden. Standing by the window in Hinde Street I made a promise to myself that I would have at least one real adventure each year, when I would come close to the things I love.

Boats have always held a fascination for me, and at one time I enrolled at evening class for a Royal Yachting Association coastal navigation course. However, for someone who has to quell rising panic when he even so much as glances at a bus timetable, I was soon struggling and then drowning as the mathematics rose up to meet me. I still don't know why I should find simple mathematics so difficult. There have been many management meetings when I have had to ask someone to remind me yet again how to read the management accounts. Not what conclusions do we draw from them, much more basic than that. The RYA course had dented my confidence but I had a friend called Pete who lived up in Penmon on Mona and he could read a bus timetable. We spoke on the phone and he enthused about the idea of a voyage out to St Kilda in the western Atlantic. I began visiting chandlers and browsing the travel section of bookstores, imagining myself on the high seas. Pete had a friend who had a 22-foot catamaran and he believed his friend would lend it to us.

Things were working out. Pete had skippered a boat to Norway and sailed around Ireland's west coast. The stories accompanying these voyages had always sounded hair raising and knowing Pete I did wonder whether he was an entirely safe companion, but then safety was not high on my agenda right then.

Pete's friend came through. The boat was somewhere 'up north' apparently and all was well. I continued to prepare, mostly by settling in my armchair and reading a shelf full of voyages undertaken by single-handed sailors. Later the following summer, and one week before we were due to set off, I called Pete again to check exactly where I should aim for to find our boat. He told me that there had been some hitches and that the owner had moved the catamaran to the Llyn Peninsula in North Wales. This was a disappointment. With the time we had available there was no way we would have time to get to St Kilda and back. Also, it was Wales, and I had left Wales hurt and angry. It didn't please me to be crossing the border again even if it was further south than the area I had previously known as home. We decided to sail for Ireland and to some extent I was mollified. Then, the night before I left London Pete called.

'The owner's moved the cat again.'

'Wha ...? ... Why?'

'I don't know, but it's okay, we can still get to Ireland.'

'Where is it then?'

'Bangor.'

'Bangor!'

'Yes.'

I wasn't happy. Bangor epitomised everything I had left Wales for. My response was not reasonable, Bangor was probably the same as it had always been, but I had had such a profoundly unhappy experience with that part of North Wales in my last two years there that it made no difference. I had also cut all ties with most of those dearest to me, and I hadn't seen them for several years.

'There's more.' It was Pete's voice again, sounding sepulchral and disembodied. I waited.

'It's moored just outside Sheila's house.'

Sheila and I had been married during the late 1970s. It had not endured, but she had remained a dear friend. Then during my last couple of years in Wales we had become estranged. I hadn't seen her for at least four years. We had shared so many experiences, many of them while at Loughborough when the dreams of a better world were exploding through the consciousness of so many young people. I had not talked to her about why I was no longer in contact. I just went quiet and slipped away.

The following day Pete and I arrived down at the small shipyard where Sheila had her house close to the water by the Menai Straits. It was still dark and I moved around like a thief. I tucked my car into a shadowed corner of the yard and grabbed my bags. We rowed the dilapidated tender out to the catamaran and climbed aboard. It was frugal, damp, and very cramped. I was beginning to have doubts about the viability of the whole project. The bilges were awash and the boat seemed a lot smaller than I had imagined. Nevertheless I was relieved that we had made it on board without being detected. The wind was strengthening from the south-west and even here in the straits it was choppy. Pete muttered something about provisions and emptied a sack of tinned beans, instant coffee and white sliced bread onto the table. Nothing felt quite right.

We untied from the mooring buoy and motored out towards the mouth of the straits. By this time the wind was up to a gale force 6 and Ireland was a long way away. Sails were hoisted and our cat leapt to the chase. It was exhilarating. We'd been sailing for about two hours, tacking up and down while we familiarised ourselves with the boat. Hard on the wind there was an almighty crack and the mast, together with the rigging and sails, rained down on us. The cabin roof was smashed in and what a few seconds previously had looked presentable, if not a little unkempt, was now a wreck. Pete, who for the most part is a very laid-back, nonchalant, and relaxed character, suddenly became very animated and began barking orders at me as we attempted to free the engine and bring the boat back under control. For my part I was relieved that Pete seemed to be taking the situation seriously and was doing my best to make sense of the nest of steel cable that was strewn across the length of the boat. As we frantically worked to get the engine started a boat rounded the headland and set a course straight for us. It was the Moelfre lifeboat. Ropes were thrown and made secure and we were steadily towed inland, eventually coming to rest on Moelfre beach. As the tide continued out we finished the day sat on the wreck that had been Pete's friend's pride and joy, and watched the sun go down.

It was decided that I should hitch-hike to Bangor to get the car so that we could begin to take some kind of action. It was clear that we were not going to be doing any sailing on this occasion but we still had the shattered remains of the catamaran to take care of. Staring out of the window at the sea on the way to Bangor, I was relieved that we were safe, very relieved that the stay had broken while we were still close to land, and happy with our brief adventure. Keeping a sharp lookout I made my way across the yard and jumped into the car. As I put the key in the ignition I noticed a note under the windscreen wiper.

'I can't believe that you're going to get this close and not knock on my door – Love, Sheila.'

Somehow the whole ridiculous fiasco seemed to make sense. I had come to see Sheila. I missed her but I couldn't admit it to myself. The elaborate arrangements, the bizarre twists and turns, my crazy efforts at avoiding detection. I got out of the car again and walked the few steps to her door and then paused before knocking. It was a big step. It wasn't the final chapter in a romantic novel. It was bigger. It was two people who were friends and who had become separated by one person's failure to be true to himself. When she came to the door I felt very stupid and I wondered how I had ever allowed this situation to develop. We had been so close; we knew each other so well. Friends are too valuable to be neglected and then left as if they have no meaning.

Later that day another friend, John Coppock, towed the catamaran back to harbour with his fishing boat and we caught mackerel on the journey. As daylight receded a group of friends sat by a barbecue, close by the water, eating fish, telling stories, making music, and sharing companionship. I don't think that the goddesses and gods usually have time to arrange such complex and minutely planned serendipitous meetings, and in any case it also feels like a colossal waste of their time.

Walking the Invisible Path, even as a conscious choice, always involves plenty of foolishness. We are not educated to this end, and our movements are clumsy and unco-ordinated. The clarity of our perception and the depth of our self-knowledge is put to the test. Whatever we perceive as unaligned to our choice tends to be rejected, and this includes friends. The glue that holds people close is not designed to withstand the imperative of changing priorities. Neither does it take account of ignorance. People, places, circumstances, ideas, perceptions, all give way to make room for the new, if not necessarily for the better. I have not met many people able to negotiate this delicate time with sensitivity, and even less with wisdom. Epiphany can come at a high price, and families seem to suffer most. Sometimes, however, we have to walk alone and find our way without support. Sometimes we're just not good at asking for help. It was with huge relief, and some embarrassment that I resumed my friendship with Sheila.

A year or two later I managed to cadge a trip across the Irish sea from Cork to Brighton. It was a mistake really. The boat seemed to be made almost entirely of fibreglass and stainless steel. I couldn't relate to it. I like a different kind of boat, something with style – iron, wood, tar, rust, that kind of thing. Twelve hours out of Cork we were slopping through a lumpy, disagreeable swell. I was feeling queasy, and an atmosphere of torpid introspection had descended on the boat. There was a piercing scream and one of the crew seemed to levitate whilst pointing to port, with an expression of ghastly foreboding etched on his terrified features. Erupting out of the water only forty feet off and boring towards us was a whale. Nobody reacted very well in the first instance. It was shocking, intimidating and awe-inspiring. There seemed to be no limit to this creature as it revealed itself metre by metre and then sounded just a few feet from the side of the yacht. Within seconds other whales appeared, spouting, curious – then gone. Silence. That's how it is. We get the chance and then it's gone; we were there, or we missed it.

Isle of Erraid Journal – 6

The wind heaves against the red door of Pier cottage, vibrating the door post and sending small shudders through the dark, warm room in which I write. The rain, driven by a north-easterly, forces its way under the window sill and spills onto my desk in tiny rivulets of chill, fresh water. Behind me the Rayburn stove toils on, taking the trees that I feed her and returning them to heat and light. Three days of electricity cuts and a wood supply that is losing ground against the fiery consumption of my stove ... All of this, and I would change none of it. I walk on the Atlantic beach each day. I go to the stone that Robert Louis Stevenson prayed with years ago, I visit the cave down at the foot of the cliffs, I live in a world of words and images, and sometimes I just have to shout with joy and life-energy. I am in a ceremony with my Self and I am drawing as deep on the Well as I can.

Every day I have to meet fear. It's as if nothing has been done or achieved up to this point. Every day it's 'Yes, but what shall you do today? Is there anything there, or is the well dry?'

I gulp, wondering if yesterday was a dream, or maybe just luck. So I walk out again on this wet and windy and grey day and I go in search of inspiration for today, knowing that if/when I get it, it will be the same tomorrow.

Erraid: Balfour Bay

The Labyrinth, Pathways' adopted logo until 2002, describes an archetypal journey. There is a desire for journey inside each one of us. It is in our DNA, and our essence as spiritual beings. All true journeys take us into unknown territory and because of this we meet ourselves — our longings, fears, joys, cowardice and courage. There are good days when we imagine that it will always be good, and bad days when we imagine that we shall be forever ground down. There are the days when we can find our heart and speak fluently about what matters to us, and at other times it is unendurably hard to find one single word. We are crushed and hide away amongst the endless rituals and conventions that our culture offers to keep us drugged and insensible. The commitment to journey always heralds a renewal, and the avoidance of journey signals that we are ready to die. If, as sometimes happens, life intervenes and lobs us into the fire then at that moment we confront a choice. Co-operate or complain. Co-operation does not mean that we passively accept our lot. It means we engage with the meaning of the time and become curious concerning our response. At best, complaining only buys us a little time. At worst we miss the richness and opportunity of a lifetime, and sometimes the life itself.

If we do not journey, we stand still. If we stand still, we atrophy. There is little middle ground.

The earth herself journeys. She is a great mentor for those that will listen. She risked the challenge of childbirth, invested millions of years in raising her human children, and now endures the challenge of teenage indifference. She cannot stop the experiments with dangerous drugs or fast cars. She has chosen to honour her promise — the gift of choice. Yet she is not the mother to endure destruction at the hands of these same children. Although risking deep hurt she will survive and she has many more millions of years before she gives herself back to essence, and another planet takes on the immense challenge of birthing life.

If we gaze upon the labyrinth, gaze within it, what do we observe and take note of that instructs us concerning its meaning? In some way, some form, the labyrinth exists for every generation of human beings across all cultures – the pathway from ignorance to knowledge, the alchemy of learning. If we dare to think deeply upon such matters, we have, of necessity, to be confronted with our ignorance. Ah now, how can that be so? I am educated. I am civilised. I am ... Every time a human being chooses to engage with the labyrinth she or he risks a confrontation and much more besides. So often journeys are circular. They lead us back to the place of beginnings, and sometimes that place has changed. It has endured the heat of the crucible and become transformed. It has become profound. Something wondrous has occurred. We have been embraced by the circle and penetrated her truth.

> We shall not cease from exploration
> And the end of our exploring
> Is to arrive at the start
> And to know it for the first time – T S Eliot

Trace the path described by the labyrinth. You will see that in moving towards the centre we are at times travelling outwards. The sense of moving away from our goal may cause our resolution to falter. Here the hidden places are to be found; here we meet both the enemies from within and those that we more readily name as other people, events, or worse, life itself. Yet this process of failure and success, disappointment and triumph, is fundamental to the acquisition of real learning. Furthermore, when have we ever chosen to learn anything of importance without an imperative that demands our attention?

So, armed with the dream that nourishes our courage, we set forth, and the pathway, so obligingly, leads us towards the centre – until the first of the four gateways – until then. Then we meet the second challenge – the first was taking the beginning step – and the real work begins. We may meet loneliness, and boldness slips between our fingers. The pathway, scorched and burnt, curves away from the centre and we find ourselves in a vortex that threatens to spin us until dizzy and we become disoriented. This is the time when we define ourselves to ourselves, and to the world around us. This is the first place of reckoning – but not with, or to, others, not with some 'other', but with and within ourselves. Four times we confront the path as it curves away from our longing. Four times we have to dig deep and find our self-honesty. Four times we are challenged to remember what started us on this path in the first place, and four times we meet the joy of a challenge well met. What are these four gateways? I think they are the four great powers that shape us, the four powers of the Self.

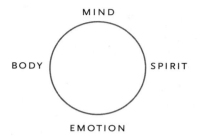

The journey of the labyrinth is the journey of self-responsibility and self-command. It is a journey that calls us to balance.

The labyrinth is no place for slaves.

The labyrinth is the Invisible Path.

Shortly before the winter break of 1993, Pathways was facing the usual cash-flow tensions that accompanied December and January. Our offices were near Marylebone High Street in London's West End and I had just returned from the gym. It was raining and I had hurried along the pavement dodging the Christmas shoppers, wondering whether or not to renew my membership. As I sat at my desk and leaned back, summoning the courage to take another look at my 'to do' list, the phone rang and I had a conversation that was to lead to friendships that have, literally, changed my life. A few days later I went along to an office located near the Lloyds building not far from Tower Bridge and provided some information on psychometric testing. We had a stimulating and humorous conversation and I walked away with a proposal to write that, if successful, would clear Pathways' monthly overheads for a year. Five years later they were still one of our principal clients and as a company they were spectacularly successful. D P Mann UA was sold and with a generosity unrivalled in my experience of the business world, David Mann, supported by his friend and co-founder Robert Mackenzie, gave everybody in the company, a share in their good fortune. Everybody did extremely well out of it and yet, perhaps predictably, remarkably few believed that they had received enough. The dissatisfaction was never really to do with the amount received, but how this figure reflected their value in comparison to others. Experience is the great fire in which we can learn, but without self-reflection experiences just pile one on top of the other and we remain none the wiser. As unformed as the child sitting next to his brother, endlessly weighing the value of his gifts on the basis of whether they are better or worse than his sibling. I too was a beneficiary of David and Robert's generosity. As our friendship deepened I had revealed more of what lay behind my work with them, and perhaps in recognition of values that they believed deserved support, and as a thank-you for my work in assisting their success, I was asked a question.

'What do you need?' David asked. 'Land,' I answered, and he wrote me a cheque for £250,000.

'It's yours. You can blow it if you wish. Go to Vegas, whatever. But, if as we think, you choose to bring some of the ideas you've spoken of into form, then we'd like to be involved and you can consider this a down-payment.'

About a year later, Azul picked up a letter that had arrived with the morning's post. I was in Poland. It was a few pages describing a property of fifty acres in Devon called Embercombe, and she called me, excited, tense, wondering. At £520,000 it was twice as much as we had, yet for some reason we pressed ahead. As I walked through Embercombe's woods with Harry, listening to his sales pitch, enjoying his hyperbole and observing how little he knew about his own back yard, I found it hard not to hug him and say, 'Yes, we'll take it. It's ours.'

I drove off and called David. He had mentioned that if I found somewhere a little more expensive I should call him and discuss it.

'David, I'm in Devon. Just been to a very beautiful place – woods, lake, meadows, airstrip, hangars ... '

'Hangars?'

'Yes. One of the previous owners was an ex-Second World War fighter pilot and he built himself his own airstrip.'

'How much is it?'

Pause, as I prevaricate, knowing it's hopeless and reluctant to let it all go so soon.

'£520,000.'

'I think it's a step too far, Mac. Sorry, but you'd better keep looking. It's out there somewhere. You'll find it.'

The phone went dead and me with it. I regretted calling him so soon. I could have enjoyed the fantasy a few hours longer at least. Later that day the phone went again.

'Is it really that beautiful ... ?' And I knew we were in with a chance.

The dream that became Embercombe was born quite a long time ago now. I was still at Loughborough College, steeped in the blazing, accelerating excitement that was the extraordinary shift in consciousness that held many millions of young women and men at that time. Much that now sits at the forefront of leading-edge social, environmental and technical innovation, and that we now take for granted, was given the most phenomenal boost at this time. It was a time of visions, Vietnam, civil rights marches, and we believed that the old world was cracking down the centre. It was, but the naivety of the time was as big as the dreams and the ugliness those dreams confronted. Drugs had arrived big-time and many alive now as leaders of our biggest organisations got just as high as the rest of us. The folk that smoked but didn't inhale were not around then, and if we are truthful there are many who in the maelstrom of an LSD trip glimpsed the vision that later fuelled their commitment to some contemporary mainstream causes; I was one such person. There are many others who were broken by the removal of the safeguarding filters which all such drugs effect upon the user. It was a lottery, and a very dangerous one. Also true is the devastating, corrupting nightmare that drugs then became when criminal big business moved in and exploited the market. The broken dream of the early seventies spawned the punk era and while a refreshing shot of gritty realism did the soft-centred dreamers no harm, it offered nothing in exchange. So we move on and everything is still to be won.

I first consciously conceived the idea of land as spiritually significant when it was vividly asserted in my imagination by Grace Slick and Paul Kantner's *Sunfighter* album. It was an epiphany. From that point to this I have had to fight my way though so many mirages, self-deceptions, tough and beautiful times. Perhaps others could have made the journey with far less collateral damage, but I couldn't. A substantial number of those I made that journey with became lost along the way. Several died, many hurt themselves badly, quite a few gave up. No matter how lost I became at certain stages over the years, the determination to find my authentic self and my true work remained a bright flame.

At my lowest point I was sitting in a flat somewhere on a housing estate in south London and the atmosphere was tense and volatile. The room was thick with smoke and a shadeless lamp lay on its side casting an abrasive, uncompromising light on the people who sat packed together around the walls. There was a lot of shouting, a couple of people had covered up their ears, one was rocking forwards and backwards reeling from the amphetamines that streamed and screamed through his veins. I sat very still, watching. There was a commotion opposite me and one guy lunged to his feet waving a revolver around and threatening to blow us all away. He looked so deranged that I tended to believe him. I remember sitting there absorbing the situation and experiencing exhilaration, shock and depression simultaneously. I was exhilarated with the drama, danger, and unpredictability of the situation, shocked at having just lost an awful lot of someone else's money, and depressed because I knew that I was sliding towards a place which was the antithesis of my dreams, hopes and aspirations. For a few more hours I remained in the deluded madness of this drama as 'The Firm' supposedly staked out airports and sea ports. Dick, the key figure, was under deep suspicion of being implicated in the heist, and I can still see his lugubrious, careworn face reassuring me that it would all work out in the end. It did, of course, for me. I walked out of that world never to return, but Dick died a year or two later, though not before pulling off one more successful scam.

The flame that was sparked in me as Grace Slick powered through that album was the knowledge that our earth is sacred and that respect, reverence, service and love are the only authentic response that I can offer in return.

I was inspired by the knowledge that:

* it is what we call our 'environment' that sustains all living beings, including humans
* life, all life, is precious and deserves respect
* freedom and equality in race and gender are fundamental principles that must not be compromised, only celebrated
* imagination, self-responsibility, courage and determination can combine to build a future that is worthy of this gift of life.

Out beyond ideas of right and wrong doing
there is a field.
I will meet you there. — Rumi

April 6th 1999, Embercombe, my new home and my first morning. I woke with a start. Seconds later I was standing upright in front of the bathroom washbasin, staring at my reflection in the mirror. I then drew my second breath. There was a moment of suspended silence and a stillness expanded around me. No-one else in the house. Alone. Alone inside this huge gift of land. For some years I had been living in a narrowboat in Little Venice, London, and the comparison in space and reach was hard to absorb. I felt like the child who stands before their first big gift, uncomprehending, lost for words. Moving slowly now and relishing each moment I descended the stairs to the kitchen and made coffee. Then carrying it to the front door I undid the latch and stepped outside, and the full weight of this magical combe rushed to meet me. I was assaulted by birdsong, by the tropical intensity of late spring in Devon, by the busyness of countless millions of beings engaged with life. With each second I felt myself go deeper into the mystery of the garden's presence. The birds, and then the trees, the wild geese, the flowers, the insects, then the impact of grass growing, drinking in the soft sunlight, the earth itself, pulsing warm and fragrant, the rocks, water, air. I have never felt so rich in all my life. For an hour or more I sat intermittently on the small wall by the open door, or walked amongst the gardens that curved around the southern and eastern aspects of the house. At one point something must have jogged my attention because I suddenly became aware of all the acres that stretched on out of sight. I hurried over towards the lake and arriving there was once again shocked into stillness. Damselflies, dragonflies, hover flies, many others I don't know, geese, ducks, moorhens, and the knowledge that so much more remained hidden to my eyes. As I stood taking it all in I felt the responsibility that I carry for this little-big piece of earth.

I think it was the overwhelming sense of things growing and multiplying that prompted me to return abruptly to the house searching for one of the few tools that I had brought from London. Rummaging amongst boxes and bags I found a spade and triumphantly went outside again. I had a vague sense that I had better get to work. With twenty acres of woodland, a lake, small stream, gardens, twenty-five acres of pasture, and an airstrip complete with three hangars, I advanced on Embercombe brandishing my spade and searching for the first task. It wasn't difficult to find something that needed doing, but it was extremely difficult to decide which should be undertaken first. For some unfathomable reason I started digging; fairly randomly as I recollect. For what reason I don't know, but it didn't last long. I felt young again, like a child rushing onto an immense sweep of beach and randomly selecting a place to dig. Twenty minutes of hard work saw me pause and lean on the spade handle as I took breath. My gaze shifted up from the ground and once again I was consumed by the erupting fecundity that hummed and buzzed in every nook. I straightened and the spade fell to the earth as my fingers uncurled, and without any conscious thought I wandered towards and into the woodland. I would take a few steps, stop, listen, and stare. I felt the tree's curiosity and, awe-struck, would take another few steps before stopping again. Another two hours passed before I re-emerged from the green-drenched temple of this woodland. Altered, and beginning a process of revelation that continues to this day, I stood looking across what we have now come to call Mary's field, after Mary Wollstonecraft. I could see a great deal, and at that moment I forgot about my spade and started thinking more in terms of a tractor.

It is nearly seven years since that day and I have been confronted the whole way with the challenge of bringing a dream into a practical working reality. I was shocked by the size of this challenge and its complexity. Before Embercombe arrived I thought I was quite clear on how I would use such a piece of land should I ever manage to secure it, but returning later in the evening to pick up the spade where I'd dropped it some hours before, it felt daunting. People visited and almost all loved the place. They were impressed, and they would ask questions. Lots of questions, such as:

* who will come?
* where will they stay?
* where will they eat?
* what will they come for?
* how will it work financially?
* is it your company, Pathways, that will run Embercombe, or a trust, or what?
* who will live here?
* who will look after the land?
* will you have animals?
* have you got planning permission?
* what will you do if you don't get planning permission?
* what's it about anyway?

I did my best to answer all of them, occasionally employing much more improvisation than I felt comfortable with. The truth was that I needed to arrive first. I had been one hundred percent involved in Pathways since 1989 and I was tired. I needed to find myself again, and I desperately needed to spend time asking myself another list of questions, such as:

* what have I achieved so far?
* why do I feel so unfulfilled?
* why am I feeling so uncertain and unsure?
* I have somewhere between zero and thirty years of work left in me. What am I going to do with this time?
* where is the love that I would like, and need, in my life?
* what is this hunger that drives me to search deeper?

Pathways, both in the UK and in Poland, was doing well. In recent times, however, this was not really my doing, since I had known for a couple of years that it was time I pulled away from running the business and sought some kind of renewal. Giving myself the chairmanship I now had time to reflect and plan, and it was not what I had imagined. The term 'spirit in business' had come to me and I was groping in the dark for what this might mean, and how it might work. Meanwhile I did the one thing that I knew would help me come to grips with the second list of questions. I went back to the garden and I spent months working in Embercombe's fields, in the woods, and around the lake. Then in October 2001 a bombshell hit when Chris, Pathways' managing director, announced his intention to leave the company. I suspect it had been brewing for months, if not longer, and on some level I was aware of it and had been trying to secure the situation. It didn't work. At the very moment when I thought I saw a future clarity, the business dissolved and my plans went with it. Chris was one of a very few experienced consultants remaining in Pathways, and he had used his immense talents in personally developing a portfolio of clients and projects that lifted the company to new heights. It had been apparent to us all that we were very exposed, but insufficient effort had been put into securing new people to replace those that had moved on. With me effectively out of the business for several years the whole thing was fractured by his departure. Out of that experience came much hardship and immense good. As events took their course, amongst other things I resolved to write, and produced an article called 'Spirit in business' in August of 2002. The article is not long, but the effort it took to locate, identify, and articulate this phrase was enormous.

2001 and my business imploded. In terms of cash reserves we were better off than we had ever been but we all knew that Pathways had been dealt a body blow and was unlikely to recover without a huge effort. I found myself in a lay-by off the A419 highway near Stroud in England, staring out across some unknown valley that I will probably never visit again, and seeing nothing. I felt numb. I had withdrawn from the day-to-day operation of the company for two years as I searched for ways to articulate a new vision – spirit in business. The company I had created in 1989 financed my introspection, and it had felt good at last to be working outside again planting an orchard, and taking some much needed time to reflect. Sitting in my parked car with traffic sweeping by relentless and disinterested, I faced the prospect of picking up the pieces and starting again. The prospect didn't appeal. Not because I shy from challenge but because the spirit that built that business had departed some time ago, and without renewal it was only a matter of time before the masonry began to crumble. Easy to see now – in retrospect. Perhaps I had averted my eyes so as not to see so well. By the time I had left that lay-by behind, physically and emotionally, something very wonderful was emerging. The vision that had swirled unformed in my imagination and subconscious for the last year or so was now taking shape. I felt a surge of excitement – a tremor, a sense of the mist drawing back, offering a glimpse of home and the flickering dance of the hearth fire. The mist closed in again, but just receiving that one vivid picture had been enough. I knew I was close, and that I would find my way.

At the same time an event of enormous significance unfolded 2,000 miles away in New York. Terrifying and shocking, a huge gaping wound, a scream so loud it reverberated around the world. Unseen, unheard, unreported, equally terrifying, just as shocking – somewhere out there, another few thousand people stopped breathing and stepped through the Life Death door, thankfully released from the agony of starvation and poverty. The forgotten, the already dead.

I understand that we are all regularly deluged with images of imminent catastrophe. Paradoxically the effect of twenty-four hour news is to deaden our concern and the need to respond. Impending crises queue for a place on the front page. It is normal, and we're used to it. In order to move forward with our own lives we take to wearing protective shields, look the other way and go deeper into pretence. I need to risk bouncing off your shield because I want to explore this pretence of ours before offering a way forward that does not rely on belief or the discredited attitudes that have created so many of our current challenges. Stay with me.

September 11th, the emergence of Corporate Social Responsibility and the anti-globalisation movement, fair trade initiatives, environmental degradation, Enron, WorldCom, the huge disparities in wealth that are growing ever larger and more dangerous – whether described as symptomatic of the problem or as emerging positive responses, we are surrounded by the signs of crisis and the need for fundamental change. We have to do what has so far proved impossible for us to contemplate. We have to square up to the shocking truth that we are systematically destroying the capability of our planet to sustain life, and that, absurdly poetic and abstract as it may seem to some, we are indeed part of life, and therefore also threatened. It is not abstract. It is fact. Organisations, structures, values, attitudes and beliefs that have sustained our outlook and way of life for generations, centuries even, are, one way or another, set to die. Meanwhile the party goes on. We take, consume, and spread our filth upon the feast we love to gorge on – but not for long. Cancer doesn't seem to accept feudal privilege. Foul air gives even rich kids asthma. We are, in effect, bent upon an act of mass suicide – and we'll succeed – unless we find the courage to truly look at what we have so far ignored, jettison our ingrained conformist acceptance of those in 'authority', and insist, demand, lead, change.

The world of business holds within it some of the best and the worst of which we are capable. Never shy of the latest fashion, we've had upsizing, downsizing, we've hammered quality nearly to death, made visions, set off on missions, and pretended the whole time that we know what we're doing. It cannot have escaped everybody's notice, however, that we also demonstrate a number of symptoms that, studied from a clinical point of view, are at the least alarming, and probably profoundly dangerous. Many times actions that would be considered brutal if promulgated by an individual are passed off as 'normal business practice' when emerging from the boardroom of organisations.

The logic advocating change is compelling, yet some still want more proof. Strange how quick we are to judge and condemn when it suits our plans, and so punctiliously anal when faced with evidence that implies our culpability. A symbol of capitalism is devastatingly destroyed and several thousand lose their lives. Every day thousands more starve. The one is personal and close to home, the other far removed, or so we choose to think: not our responsibility, not our business. The one lives as a symbol of everything upon which we stack our dreams, the other is a hideous nightmare that we strive to suppress.

We in business still persist in seeing work as separate from life, separate from 'commercial realities', separate from my niece's birthday or the small bird outside my window hopefully scanning the bird table for food. All life is connected and in relationship. It is time that we accepted the obvious.

We need clever leaders, but much more importantly we need wise ones. We need power to come together with ethics. We need to care about profits and my niece, about commercial realities and the small bird outside my window. Not one at the expense of the other. Of course we need to drive for performance, rewarding initiative, energy and enterprise but we need to pursue our business goals while also understanding that in doing so we are the architects of tomorrow. We compromise our values at the risk of forgetting that we owe the present to the past, and the future to the present.

Without a rapid and profound shift in the beliefs, attitudes and assumptions that guide current business practice, we may lose the spectacular opportunity that now presents itself for positive and radical change. None of us can plead ignorance. Somehow we have to rise to the challenge – put aside cynicism, put aside self-doubt, learn to play again, have an adventure – and do what needs to be done. We are all responsible and we are all culpable. Why can't we enthusiastically support businesses in their efforts to trade successfully, make profits, and prosper, and yet absolutely reject the thesis that this can be done in the absence of a moral or ethical framework that celebrates human rights, cares for our environment, embraces social responsibility, and takes pride in so doing? These issues will present themselves increasingly to every one of us and somewhere down the line we will each have to make a choice on where we stand.

Until we rediscover reverence for life, for our Earth, for all the beings with whom we share our lives; until we perceive mystery without then needing to deny science; until we elevate rational thought without needing to denigrate spirit; until we set about our own personal development as human beings - seeking wisdom, growing compassion, healing ourselves of beliefs that are hurtful to ourselves and to others - we will never attain true freedom and our world will lurch deeper into crisis.

We have to grow wise fast. Spirit moves in us all. It is what brings us joy and urges us to strive for meaning and purpose in our lives. Spirit inspires you and me to be generous, to gasp at the huge presence of the ocean, to search for love in our lives, to dig deep and seek the very best of which we are capable. Spirit is not confined or defined by dogma, beliefs, churches or cults. Spirit should not be confused with religion. Spirit is you and I growing our gardens with tenderness and appreciation; it is the young child climbing her first tree; it is the huge leaping joy of birth, and the final embrace of someone we love. Spirit guides our greatest dreams and accompanies us in the darkest moments of loneliness. Spirit is the inspiration of all that is beautiful in you, and in me. In spirit we rediscover reverence for life, and perceive the meaning we long for.

How has it ever come to pass that we should be embarrassed to say or feel such things? How is it right that our business leaders - people who are chiefs to thousands of other humans - talk so little of things important either to their own families or the families of those they affect indirectly or directly - which is you and me, all of us - around the world.

All organisations seek ways of motivating their employees to give more; with passion and energy to pursue goals that will benefit the organisation. I think that we can motivate people to a point by using conventional incentives but beyond this we have to connect to their own deeply held ideals. This is what is fuelling those who fight for our rainforests, our oceans, our human rights. There is a huge opportunity waiting for companies that are brave enough to name values that truly relate to the dreams and hopes of ordinary people worried about the world that we are so busy destroying. Most governments are failing to meet this challenge. They espouse peace and yet enthusiastically trade in arms, they talk of the environment and drag their feet in actually doing anything about it. Business is the power house of change, but if this is to be positive, constructive change, then our business leaders need to become much braver, more radical, more determined to lean into the wind and insist upon change. We must stand in awe of beauty, accept the challenge of our own self-learning, and be brave enough to stand up and be counted.

This is the stuff of leadership. It is born from inspiration, and from a vision of leadership that is, at its essence, spiritual. I see a clear difference between spiritual and religious. The former I have described above and concerns a respect and reverence for life, the latter concerns belief. We do not have to believe in a tree, or believe in the beauty of our earth. We have only to look up and see what exists around us. Our brightest and best leaders will find such visions if they are encouraged to touch the lives of ordinary people, and to see for themselves the destruction that accompanies corporate business activity when it resists any kind of moral framework. They will find such visions when they spend time in reflection asking themselves questions that are profound and universal:

What is of true value? What is my relationship to life, and what are the responsibilities that I carry? What do I perceive as my purpose and what gives meaning to my life? These gifts that are mine – how shall I use them? Who are my children — what are my responsibilities to them? Of what can I truly be proud when the time comes for me to die?

Some months ago I sat by a lake listening to the sounds that accompany the onset of dusk. The geese had flown in a few minutes before, and the trout were lazily taking the evening mosquitoes. The last swallows skimmed the water and the first owl called out, beckoning the dark. I felt skinless, raw - touched by beauty. I felt wealthy. This lake is well known to me, friends visit and almost all are in some way touched. It is confronting to meet beauty. It is confronting to meet life. No 'belief' is necessary, just an openness and sensitivity to colour, scent, light, warmth, music, and the poetry that is whispered in the reflected images of clouds.

As the dark cloaked itself around the lake, my thoughts turned to the many remarkable people my colleagues and I have met over the last thirteen years of trading - the laughter, the wisdom, the generosity. None of us gets there on our own. At every stage life brings us allies, guides, teachers and friends. There are many people in business who choose to direct their brilliance, energy and resourcefulness to finding solutions for the huge problems that now confront us. It is hope we need, and hope is to be found in each other. This is my work for the coming years – to do all in my power to contribute to this time of decision and action – to be with hope. As a young man I was so sad to have been born at a time when adulthood only seemed to offer the dreary safety of a planned career, a hefty mortgage and a plump pension. I am so glad I got that one wrong.

Later, on the same day that I had sat in my parked car trying to re-adjust and find a way forward, I arrived home in south Devon. I was shocked at how easily I had moved from angry paralysis to excitement and purpose. Standing in the garden I took a deep breath, tasting the flavours of wood smoke, newly turned earth and the damp Atlantic breeze. It felt good to be alive. It still took most of the winter months to claw the vision of 'spirit in business' from the half-formed intuitions that hovered like shadows, dancing just out of sight. But a vision once seen is not so easily forgotten, and like the kingfisher that just now has blazed her blue fire across the lakeside waters, I have work to do.

This article was never formally published. I couldn't interest the magazine editors I approached. Looking for other ways of sending it out into the world, I offered it to Niall Fitzgerald, at that time Unilever's co-Chairman, and from that point it began to take on a life of its own. Writing this article had a profound effect on me. When I finished it I knew where I stood, and I knew what had to be done. It marked an arrival, a decision. It was a stake hammered into the ground. It did more than this. It attracted attention and in the dim light that illuminated my future I found new friends within the business world who offered me their friendship and opportunities to explore.

I stood on Blackfriars Bridge watching the traffic on the river and the strong pull of the incoming tide. It was November, bright, glistening and chill. I had forty-five minutes before going into Unilever's HQ and meeting Niall Fitzgerald. We hadn't met before and I had only a short time to register my existence in a way that might continue and build the positive relations I was cultivating with this immense business. I looked down at the river as it flooded upstream, happened to notice my shoes and inwardly groaned. It's one thing to go in to a meeting looking relaxed and casual, but 'rustic' doesn't quite work. Blackfriars is not a place to sport many shoe shops but I cut my reverie short and began to anxiously patrol the surrounding streets. It seemed oddly normal that immediately around from Unilever House there, with nothing else close by, should be a small independent shoe shop. I emerged feeling much better, and no longer suggesting from my appearance that 'spirit in business' necessarily meant a collapse in profits.

I went back to the river. I like to spend some time with the things that mean something to me before I go into meetings of this kind. It helps remind me why I choose to do this work. Just before Pathways went into free-fall in 2001 I was ambivalent about continuing to work in the same field. The only thing that drew me back was the knowledge that there is a fight to be fought and that I'm well placed to contribute. However, for reasons I explore later in this book, I had to do it on my terms. I had no choice. Spending time with the river brought me a peaceful acceptance that I was in the right place at the right time doing something that had meaning to me. If an organisation like Unilever chose to align itself behind a corporate purpose that was about contributing to the great challenges of our time, and then strove to achieve integrity in all aspects of its operation, others of equal weight and power would sit up and take notice. With everything to go for, and spending time with this great river, I felt that the shoes had been a worthwhile investment.

There is an aura that accompanies the suites of Chairmen in these big businesses, and it's fun to visit them and hang out for a while. You are treated as a kind of visiting dignitary and new shoes are cool in such surroundings. I lounged in the armchair with a coffee. It's a life I might have adjusted to quite easily if a few things had worked out a little differently. My time by the river had informed me. I had to find a way of getting close and making the time meaningful. For both our sakes we had to find a way of leaving this office and walking a beach together.

I had just come from a funeral. Fiona's family had asked me to lead a farewell ceremony for her. There would be no church service. We would gather as friends and remember the wonderful, engaging, spirited person that had been Fi. We would remember and celebrate her warmth and generosity, her curiosity, her big laugh. I had met Fi in the course of working for a client organisation. She had contracted cancer and fought over several years to stay healthy, but slowly she lost ground. She was well loved and several hundred people turned out to say goodbye. I was honoured to be asked to perform such a service. She had come to Embercombe and we had sat by the lake. She had spoken of her life, and tears had blessed our conversation. It is not right that such feelings should be held back. I was glad that she came. We were to meet more but the next time I saw her she was very ill in hospital and time was getting short. It hurts many people that they never see the value of something until it is taken away. It need not be like that. Life is so immeasurably enriched by appreciation. Now some of Fi's ashes grace the lakeside where we sat those few years ago and others have the chance to ask themselves questions that might provide illumination – while there is still time.

A friend of mine wrote to her suggesting that with the question: 'Why am I dying?' she might also ask: 'Why am I alive?' It is a question that many never ask.

'Good to meet you, Mac. So, tell me about Pathways.'

I quickly brought the river back into the forefront of my mind and followed its advice. I offered to answer the question indirectly through a question of my own.

'At the end of your life, when you stand by your grave looking back along the trail that you have left behind you ... will you be proud?'

I enjoyed that meeting. Niall Fitzgerald can be very gracious, amusing, and, I felt, sincere. He is someone you wouldn't mind spending time with, leaning on a bridge contemplating the incoming tide.

I also left heartened. I don't know whether that conversation changed anything, or strengthened anything, but I know that the river was present, and I know that I did the best I could. After that we move on, and in my case I went back to the bridge and changed my shoes. The new ones were cramping my feet.

Another brochure was produced which sent Pathways out on a new journey, and with huge support and encouragement from many friends, a new future began to emerge. Every positive step forward was preceded with gruelling effort, as I battled with a gnawing sense of self-doubt – not in the vision, but in my ability to bring it to fruition. Emphatically, once again I understood how our lives are influenced by cycles of learning and growing, which, until reconciled and integrated, return repeatedly until we deal with them. There must be many people who have experienced leaving a relationship behind them and march confidently into a new future, only to find it turn up again – this time as a new face and with a different name. We struggle to divest ourselves of some old wound and believe the matter resolved and dealt with. Years later, there it is again; looking a little different perhaps, but recognisable for all that. There are themes of learning and growing that walk with us all our lives and really it is unrealistic to believe that they can be magically spirited away, even if this is still the presiding mantra of many self-development avatars. Every step of true change is worked for. It takes time and it takes courage. When an old skin is shed we wonder what the struggle was all about, but the struggle earned us our day of victory. When so much emphasis is given to convenience and our lives lean ever more readily towards vicariousness, it is not surprising that the painful demands of true journey and direct experience are looked at askance.

I had been living with a condition that was embarrassing and sometimes debilitating. It had been going on for several years and I found it hard to accept. After years of working with groups, chairing meetings, speaking to large groups, and endless one to one meetings with the great and good, I had started to suffer from panic attacks. There was one question that seemed to spin me straight into the danger zone. It went something like this:

'So. Tell me about Pathways.'

There are people I met out there in organisations over this period of years who, reading these words, will finally find illumination for my inexplicable and occasionally bizarre behaviour. It happened during courses, in sales meetings, any place, anytime, and it would render me speechless. There would be some kind of trigger and I would experience a curious disengagement. Once started I couldn't bring myself back and I'd know that I had around thirty seconds maximum before I couldn't speak another word, literally. It led to some unorthodox behaviour on my part since I was unwilling to simply state: 'Excuse me, I'm having a panic attack and will be unable to speak in ten seconds'. I rediscovered improvisation, and became highly skilled in masking the truth of my situation – coughing fits, sudden confronting questions, 'My God, is that the time?', influenza relapses, the abrupt truncation of a story, questions that seemed wildly tangential to the context and erratically timed. I suffered, and I suspect some others did as well.

It got worse. I had to brief colleagues before meetings or courses, so that they could spot the symptoms and interject if there was a pause that seemed inconsistent with the moment. The trouble was that these attacks came arbitrarily and randomly, and since I enjoy telling a story and have a cultivated ability to measure a pause to heighten dramatic effect, there were many unnecessary and infuriating interjections. Many times I didn't know whether to weep or laugh. All of this may account for the fact that sales were sluggish and erratic. It came to a head when, after months of trying to find a way, I was kindly given the opportunity of meeting Tim Smit, the man whose inspiration lit the flame that became the Eden Project in Cornwall. I had visited Eden with Azul, and I'd read Tim's first book. I felt I had found someone with whom I shared a common understanding, a man who had drunk from the same well and was similarly inspired. Eden is only an hour down the A38 from Embercombe and I could see all sorts of possibilities that could support Eden while also assisting the new Pathways and perhaps involving Embercombe. It was a cold and wet winter's morning when I clambered up the portakabin steps to Eden's administrative offices. I was cursing the fact that I hadn't brought someone with me, but it was too late. In our kind of work meetings like this are crucially important. One champion from inside an organisation and doors open. Without an avenue to such a person the organisation remains a hostile and impregnable citadel. I could hear his voice before he entered the room. In that moment I knew that I was on the edge. It was humiliating and very tough to be so close, to know that in good form I could open this door, and yet also to know that I was precariously balanced. He entered the room, flashed me a disinterested glance, shook hands, sat opposite, leaned forward arms folded, and stared at me.

'Well?'

And I knew I had twenty seconds. I've never tried so hard in my life to speak through my fear, but I couldn't do it. I struggled, searched for words and couldn't find them, repeated myself, bored myself, lost meaning, and finally lapsed into silence and defeat. All along he just sat and stared, his face immobile, without compassion and without hostility. I don't think I've ever felt so crushed. Here I was, clutching my new vision, knowing deep in my soul that I had something precious, knowing that I had the inspiration and the energy to communicate it and make a difference, but I couldn't do it. There was a long silence and he asked me if I'd like something to drink. His previous indifference had now become concern, but he didn't patronise me for which I was grateful. It was now blatantly obvious that I was in turmoil. I managed to rally a little and briefly explained what was happening to me. I offered a question and gratefully listened as he obliged and gave me some seconds respite. It was all I needed and the remainder of the meeting passed off without further incident, only that I knew and he knew that it would lead nowhere.

There came a point when I turned and faced this thing. I began to realise that for whatever reason life was presenting me with an ultimatum, and that without effort it was not going to melt away in the same way in which it had arrived.

> 'Be authentic. Speak only from your heart, the truth as you
> best know it. Trust. Trust. Trust. All will be well. Trust. The
> Invisible Path will never betray you, but listen, listen.'

I began to realise that these attacks were associated with a rift or split within me. They were showing me something and I needed to attend closely. We don't always notice when the trail that once held so much meaning begins to lose definition, falter, and fade. It was time to pause and take stock. Somewhere, hidden within the energy sphere of every human, there is a source of wisdom that unerringly guides us to the experiences we need for the Self to grow and become conscious. The intention of the Self cannot be withstood, even though so many of us plumb extraordinary depths in our quest for an effective avoidance strategy. Some strategies can postpone the meeting – for a lifetime even – but the price is always heavy. I didn't want to avoid my Self. I wanted engagement. Yet it is often painful, even if a few steps the other side we find deep happiness. There was another feeling: embarrassment. A sense of profound discomfort. Shouldn't I be past all this by now? Shouldn't I radiate self-confidence, dignity, and gravitas? An elder, with the scars to prove it?

'Nope', answers the Self, unconcerned with questions of status, time, and delicate dispositions.

I was not aligned. Looking back now, I understand that in earlier years the task of establishing an ethical company and working with managers to assist them develop as leaders was enough. Not any more. Not for me. The events of the last few years had revealed an imperative for me to dedicate myself to work that held deeper levels of meaning for me. I no longer had the choice to do anything less. I had asked life for the opportunity to engage one of the big issues of our time. I had done my apprenticeship and now I was being given everything I needed. All that was asked was that I be my Self, as fully and deeply as I knew how. But to achieve this ... ?

I went back to the garden and I began to develop and explore several strategies for meeting myself once more and becoming strong again. I also decided to be more gentle with myself and less driven. My commitment was absolute, but first I needed to find centre and become still. The vulnerability of that time is with me still, but instead of seeking to lose it I treasure the companionship. I welcome the demand. If you kneel to the rose you must accept her beauty without seeking to ignore or remove the thorns. The thorns are beautiful also. I went back to the garden.

Isle of Erraid Journal – 7

When I walk close to the sea in this place on Erraid's west shore, when I look down to the salt water, I feel her moving amongst the rocks, seeking out the little ways, reaching into her own veins. I know that she is my own blood. I know that she travels in me, inside me, and that there is no difference, no wall of indifference. The rocks in this place are red, a deep rose pink, and I see the walls of my arteries and veins. The ocean flows amongst them. When the moon pulls and the ocean responds with the spring and neap tides I know that my blood also responds. That all water responds. That trees in their girth swell and contract and the mystery and the ceremony of the woman's moon times – all are part of this great flowing. And it is a wonder, and it never was a curse, and it always is a blessing. Once this was known, and those peoples still not infected with the belief of superstition, who know what is sacred in life, understand that it is a ceremony and a blessing, not a curse.

And don't men know the pull of the moon? Don't we also have blood in our veins, water flowing between the great oceans inside us? Don't we also feel the pull of the tides, the coming and the going and the great renewal? Of course we do. But if we have in mind that it is a curse, that life is a curse, that creation somehow screwed up and got it wrong, then we won't find it in ourselves. If we felt the slightest tremor, would we not dodge and dive away from it as something dirty, frightening, shameful? Oh yes we would, and we have. The great rivers flow inside us and the waters answer the call of the moon as they do in all other living things, which is to say, everything.

In the first year of arriving at Embercombe I planted the orchard – apples, pears, plums, cherries, walnuts, cobnuts, mulberry, quince and crab-apple. It was late February 2000 when I began and the days were short. I had selected one of the lower fields where gales from the south-west were less likely to inflict too much damage on the young trees. The grass was luxuriant and facing south it seemed ideal. Because Embercombe and the land around is patrolled by large herds of deer I knew that the field needed to be deer-fenced if the trees were to survive more than a few weeks. Deer-fencing is not cheap, and like most fences visually discordant with the land. Nonetheless it was essential, and I had plans to grow a beech hedge adjacent to the fence so that it would become lost inside the hedge as the trees became established. I designed the orchard to encompass a circular vegetable garden of about seventy metres diameter. Including the orchard the whole area occupied about three acres. The fruit trees on the perimeter of the circle were grafted on M25 rootstock which, taken together with the fruit tree variety itself, should mean they grow as full-size standard trees. Next come trees on M111 rootstock which grows half-standards, and then finally the inner trees of the circle on M106 rootstock which are semi-dwarfed. The effect I sought was that of a bowl, the trees throwing out their limbs to the sky graciously inviting the blessings of sunlight, wind and rain. The orchard that is a bowl is my promise of giving to life.

I was not prepared for the feelings that welled up within me as the work progressed. I had thought that I was the gardener and the trees were my young charges, but last summer I realised differently. I was working in the vegetable garden hoeing. It was very early in the morning and had not long been light. The sun was topping the woodland and piercing the early morning mist with long arms of warmth that caressed the unripe wheat. I was alert, present with the garden, and acutely conscious of my relationship with the combe and all her other residents. I felt that the land was becoming used to me, that I had my place and was welcome. As I wielded the hoe and moved along the rows of vegetables I began to be aware of a presence in the garden. It came quickly, like footsteps sounding along a corridor before the door opens and someone enters the room. As I straightened from my work and looked around, I knew. On some level I knew that the fruit trees had arrived, and that the balance between us had shifted. It had taken four years. I was being gardened. I was their charge. I had thought I was planting them for their benefit – restoring one more orchard to Devon's depleted heritage. I was wrong. The trees are engaged, absolutely and completely, in the same struggle that the 'Spirit in Business' article describes. For millions of years they laboured cleaning the air so that we and others could be. For millions of years they have played a crucial role in stabilising climates, CO_2 levels, water tables, water run-off, providing food and building materials, warming our homes and cooking our food. They teach us, and levy no charge. They grace our world with their beauty. All this and more. Much more. I now work in this orchard just a little more respectfully. I go there to replenish myself, to be gardened, to experience the grace that they bestow so very generously. I go there to remember what is important, and to remember myself. I go there because I love them, and because I remember them from the days of my childhood when they endured my growing up and gave me my first early lessons in balance, in confidence, in appreciation, in all things important to the young human.

To revere the earth is as natural to humans as loving their children. Both relationships naturally draw forth an appropriate expression of interdependence and gratitude. If we did not love our children they would die or grow up severely wounded and disabled, as indeed some do. It is the same with the earth. For many reasons, some complex and some starkly simple, we in the Western world have become so estranged and distant from the reality of our relationship with nature that we now imagine that we are fully independent. Physically, emotionally, intellectually and spiritually, this is untrue. Many people love their gardens. In Britain gardening is now one of our most popular leisure activities. Embercombe is being developed as a sanctuary and school where people, including those from the business world, can meet the garden once more, and mend some of the dislocated threads that have torn and separated inside us.

Not long ago an executive in charge of the ongoing personal development of a large corporation came down and spent some time with me at Embercombe. We had a good time, exchanging views, swapping information, and getting to know each other. At one stage he asserted that not everyone found inspiration in nature; that it was as easy and 'natural' to find an inspiring spiritual illumination sitting in a café in central London or any other big city.

At first this seemed very reasonable, but I later realised that it missed a larger and more fundamental truth. There are hundreds, probably thousands of ways in which people can meet a deepening sense of who they are and derive spiritual benefit. However, I think that a huge proportion of our greatest social, environmental, and economic challenges are directly or indirectly connected with our disassociation and alienation from nature, from the earth. We don't all have to be gardeners and we don't all have to love January gales on a Hebridean beach, but appreciation and respect are usually forthcoming when a direct and intimate relationship is made possible. I was scrupulously careful with the quantity of wood I used in the wood-stove on Erraid. It was me who brought the wood into the cottage, observed the stove's hunger, experienced the cold when I walked the cliffs, and luxuriated in the warmth the stove gave me on my return. Once again, as on many previous occasions I learned to appreciate trees, and value them.

It is very hard to make way for the new. We are the last of an era. Leaders everywhere are being called to see anew, and for a while most will fail. Others less encumbered with the assumptions of the past are stepping forward. Our concept and practice of leadership will undergo immense change, and the lodestar of leadership will never be the same again. Leaders will abound, but not the type that we're used to – simply women and men of vision whose dedication is not centred on themselves, or the pursuit of growth and profit, but rather the certain conviction of service: to our Earth, our non-human relatives, and all humanity. These leaders will appear and function within every society and location of our global family. It will be so, because it must be so. Held close to the heart of the people will be the ancient ecological and spiritual appreciation of the Earth that has been held safe for us by countless indigenous peoples around the world. Deep psychological and spiritual wounds inflicted upon us by beliefs that respect only greed and possession will find healing. To get there we will have to pass through various gateways, and one of the very first of these is our relationship with half of our own species, with women. We have incurred devastating consequences to the human psyche, and wrought untold harm upon the earth, by shifting ourselves so far out of balance with natural laws. Femininity and masculinity are twin expressions of spiritual laws, the laws of balance and reciprocity. The physical world illuminates and reveals the spiritual by creating forms that express and make visible the invisible spiritual framework upon which life is built. The universe, with unfathomable generosity, gave Earth precisely the right conditions for life to emerge. Our Earth then took on her own responsibilities and tirelessly, skilfully, consummately holds that balance with an intelligence and grace incomprehensible to our grandiose self-importance. In many societies around the world young boys fantasise and learn that they are in every way superior to girls. Schools, religions, governments, and organisations, all mostly agree. It must be so otherwise there would be equality. We hold the same childish, ego-driven beliefs in the way we choose to live on Earth. Celebrating, teaching, and extolling the qualities of competitiveness, dominance, control and exploitation, our society has endlessly manifested the same unleavened patriarchal brutality that has brought our civilisation so much suffering. It's time for a change.

The Invisible Path is our creation-given spiritual journey. We give this journey many different names and champion different prophets, but that is just our human way. Creation is bigger than humanity, and bigger than the human-created powers that inform us of 'God's will'. Women, and the profound mystery of the feminine, at least as far as it can be influenced by humans, have been held in slavery for several thousand years – the same timescale in fact that has seen the emergence of Islam, Confucianism, Hinduism, Judaism, Christianity and Buddhism. It was not always so. No single major religion places women equal with men. They all assert that they do, but none has equal numbers of women sitting in the highest positions of authority and direction, if indeed any. In fact, in a mostly systematic fashion, they have undermined women, and with women has gone our earth because the two are inextricably and spiritually intertwined. When a friend of mine went to Mass recently in the US, the priest was able to announce that without Christianity women would still be degraded and disempowered, and the audience of women and men enthusiastically concurred. Matilda Joslyn Gage, writing in 1893, saw it rather differently. In fact she felt so strongly about it that she dedicated years of research to the writing of *Woman, Church and State*, still now a striking indictment of Christianity's betrayal of women:

> Woman is told that her present position in society is entirely due to Christianity; that it is superior to that of her sex at any prior age of the world, Church and State both maintaining that she has ever been inferior and dependent, man superior and ruler. These assertions are made the basis of opposition to her demands for exact equality with man in all the relations of life, although they are not true either of the family, the church, or the state. Such assertions are due to non-acquaintance with the existing phase of historical knowledge, whose records the majority of mankind have neither the time nor opportunity of investigating.

> Christianity tended somewhat from its foundation to restrict the liberty of woman enjoyed under the old civilisations. Knowing that the position of every human being keeps pace with the religion and civilisation of his country, and that in

many ancient nations woman possessed a much greater degree of respect and power than she has at the present age, this subject will be presented from a historical standpoint. If in so doing it helps to show man's unwarranted usurpation over woman's religious and civil rights, and the very great difference between true religion and theology, this book will not have been written in vain, as it will prove that the most grievous wrong ever inflicted upon woman has been in the Christian teaching that she was not created equal with man, and the consequent denial of her rightful place in Church and State.*

Much has changed since Matilda Gage was writing, but far less than most people suppose:

* In England, we, that is men, only 'gave' all women (under massive sustained pressure) the vote in 1928. Or did they take it? Either way, we hung on as long as we possibly could.
* Women with as good or better qualifications than men often do not have their skills valued the same as men's and their career progression is slower. The average pay gap in the EU is 16% (European Commission's Directorate General for Justice 2013).
* Of the world's 500 largest corporations, only 13 have female Chief Executive Officers (UN Department of Economic & Social Affairs 2010).
* 70% of the 1.3 billion people living in abject poverty are women and children (UN 1997).
* 1% of the titled land in the world is owned by women (UN).

To be a woman and not to be a feminist is puzzling to me.

We are unlikely to achieve either balance or wisdom on this earth until we have restored women to full equality – in governments, in corporations, in public office, in universities, in religions. This single undertaking would signal a momentous change of consciousness, and, I suspect, move us dramatically closer to living sustainably. In relationship with life and not opposed to it.

* Matilda Joslyn Gage, *Woman, Church and State*, Watertowne MA: Persephone Press, 1980, p. 12.

Searching for traditions and spiritual philosophies that held women equal to men and honoured the Earth, we now have to look to the indigenous peoples that we so heartily despised not long ago. The Circle of Law was in existence in the Americas before the oldest established religions. As one of the very earliest forms of democracy it was birthed from a people who knew that the earth was sacred, and who eschewed beliefs in favour of an earth science that revered life while also giving us one of the greatest mathematical discoveries of all times, the zero. Central in their observations and experience of the earth was the balance within creation between male and female. The twin subjects of reverence for our earth, Creator Mother and Creator Father, and the full, unequivocal equality of women with men cannot be separated. We have to bring earth, all of nature, to the centre of our spirit consciousness because only there will we remember the debt we owe her, and only then will we be at peace with ourselves and nature. From this place of wisdom governments will form policies that will sustain and protect our earth, corporations will place sustainability and social responsibility at the centre of their business activities, universities will once again become seats of true learning and wisdom, and religions will rediscover an integrity that was set aside when control became the guiding motive.

It is worth remembering that the difficulties surrounding religion have rarely centred on the prophets who inspired them but on the churches that men created in their name. Complementary to this is the obvious truth that there are a great many wonderful individual priests, rabbis, monks and imams who have dedicated themselves to the care and well-being of their fellow humans, of all races and creeds. Extraordinary women and men exist within and without religions, always have, always will. This set aside, I do not think that it is to religions that we should look for the re-balancing of our earth, because they have been so deeply implicated in its unbalancing. Neither should we look to science as it is expressed in the old Cartesian/Newtonian mechanistic model. For all the wonders revealed to us by traditional science, it has suffered from the lack of a spiritual integrity and social morality. Because science quickly revealed the crude mendacity of the medieval Christian Church, it has stumbled on like an adolescent child, pumped up with egotism, and fast assuming all the worst traits of the faiths it so enthusiastically and mercilessly trounced. It seeks to become a religion itself. The bullied becomes the bully.

A new science is emerging. It rejects the old religious superstitions, the misinformation, and the scientific dogma. It meets the subject of its study, life and her laws, with awe and reverence. There is no need to war against ways of thinking and being that are already dissolving and announcing their departure, but there is a need for scholars to dig underneath the lies and pretences that have obscured so much of the human story. It is necessary because so much of our received history has been given to us by the same people who wished to cover up the tracks, and it has left us disconnected with our past, our ancestors, and our traditions.

The sacredness of the growing seed, the flowering rose, birdsong, water, all the gifts of Earth, are easily appreciated by those raised to respect nature, the life-bringer. Religion finds it very hard to accept dissent; when in the ascendant it usually responds by threatening punishment upon unbelievers, and obstructing all true critical and rational thinking. This is the price we pay for having belief introduced into our thinking as a fundamental foundation block for a spiritual life. There is no need for belief. In fact it introduces dis-ease into us because instinctively we fear the real and present danger of fantasy and pretence. Only those already succumbing to great personal pain, sadness, ignorance, or laziness will abdicate their own thinking and substitute beliefs in their place. Religions and their churches find it hard to resist the temptation to control. We have only to hope that, as so many now seek their own authentic spiritual relationship with life, sufficient numbers will lead the way to a new confidence in spirituality without belief.

When we focus on experience and allow ourselves to look at life with the eyes and vision of the artist and poet, the mist will clear and we will know that our Earth is sacred, alive, and with powers to heal.

Whatever is true will eventually prevail. Right now we have the task of coming together as a people and working towards a solution to our huge and growing global crisis. The environmental and social symptoms that articulate this crisis are essentially an expression of spiritual ennui. They are shadows of the same pain that accompanies the loneliness of losing our way. Everything that challenges our world today is an expression of this spiritual crisis, and like all crises, it represents a time of huge opportunity in which we may claim at least the hem of wisdom's shawl.

The re-balancing of our earth, the new spirituality, is coming from us, the people, as we seek out a new relationship with life that does not require any institution, expert or go-between to interpret for us. When we can stand before creation without translators and know spirit as the in-spir-ation she/he is, we will have come of age and the earth will not fear its children.

CHAPTER FIVE

In the balance

"Crisis", I said.

"What crisis?" The question was genuine, enquiring. "Aren't you overstating the situation somewhat?"

I didn't say anything for a while. I was experiencing a sudden and dramatic shift in perspective.

Ah, I thought. I'd assumed we had moved past that one. In my ignorance I truly thought that on this, at least, we were all agreed. Not so. Many, I would even say most, of the business managers I meet and work with do not *really* believe that we face a crisis. No. It still hasn't sunk in, or it has sunk in and the waters have closed above it. Too big. Too difficult to contemplate. Too many implications, were I to let this one really make sense. So I go home and continue to think only in terms of the intimate minutiae that comprise the daily rhythms of my life, and the important organisation for which I work.

Crisis. So, a summary of current research indicating the health of our planet – an unequivocal statement of how things stand, as seen by the vast *majority* of top scientists working in these fields. There are, of course, those that hold contrary views, but they are now a small minority, and while I think their views should be heard it is with the majority that I wish to place my confidence at this late stage.

WORLDWATCH INSTITUTE*

Climate change

The Earth's atmosphere is now warming at the fastest rate in recorded history, a trend that is projected to cause extensive damage to forests, marine ecosystems and agriculture. Human communities are also threatened by climate change as seas rise, storms become more intense,

*The following information is taken from www.worldwatch.org (19/04/2006).

and episodes of drought and flooding increase. The scientific evidence is now compelling that recent climate change is caused at least in part by human activities – especially the burning of fossil fuels, which has driven atmospheric carbon dioxide concentrations to their highest level in 420,000 years.

Biodiversity

The world lives amid the greatest mass extinction since the dinosaurs perished 65 million years ago and most of this loss is caused by human activities. Habitat loss, the introduction of exotic species through trade and travel, and climate change all contribute to biodiversity decline.

Oceans

Our planet's vast oceans have been viewed throughout history as an inexhaustible resource, both in terms of what they can produce and what they can absorb. But the ecological limits of oceans became apparent in the last decade. Eleven of the world's fifteen most important fisheries, and 70% of commercial fish species are now fully exploited or over-exploited. Pollution of coastal waters often contaminates many remaining fish species.

Forests

The world has lost nearly half its forested area in the past 8,000 years, and the majority of that loss occurred in the 20th century, when cultivated areas expanded rapidly and consumption of wood and paper jumped dramatically.

Population

The human family has grown more in the last 50 years than in all of previous human history. Such rapid population growth has strained many countries' capacity to address social issues, leaving many in poverty and driving a downward spiral of economic misery.

Water

Water scarcity may be the most under-appreciated global environmental challenge of our time. In the Middle East, China, India and the United States, groundwater is being pumped faster than it is replenished, and rivers such as the Colorado and Yellow River no longer reach the sea year round. Over the next quarter-century, the number of people in countries unable to meet their domestic, industrial and agricultural water needs is expected to balloon substantially.

And just to bring it home, here's another way of putting much of the same information across. It is worth reading it a couple of times to let it sink in. Thom Hartmann was writing in 1998, which means that some years have passed between then and now. Days numbering in thousands.

> In the 24 hours since this time yesterday, over 200,000 acres of rainforest have been destroyed in our world. Fully 13 million tons of toxic chemicals have been released into our environment. Over 45,000 people have died of starvation, 38,000 of them children. And more than 130 plant or animal species have been driven to extinction by the action of humans... And all this just since yesterday.

In January 2004, Tony Blair's chief scientist, David King, wrote that climate change is a more serious threat to the world than terrorism, and added his voice to the many who know that without US cooperation our chances of success are greatly diminished. In 2013, close to completing his term in the same role, Sir John Beddington stated that "the evidence for climate change is completely unequivocal" and commented that the later governments left it, the harder it would be to control the problem. Sir Mark Walport took over as chief scientist for the government and has made clear his intention to ensure that scientific knowledge translates into economic growth. In his inaugural speech at the Centre for Science and Policy Annual Conference 2013, he gave us a hint of what this might imply by highlighting the doubtful nature of current evidence linking the crash in bee populations with the use of neonicotinoid insecticides and the need to assess the likely economic impact of withdrawing this class of pesticides. He said, "It's about how we take the extraordinary scientific base in the United Kingdom and turn this to the best economic advantage."

And there, I think, we have it. Our most educated, rational, celebrated and influential thinkers *still* place the economy ahead of *everything* else, even our future. With very few exceptions, conventional leadership is unwilling and perhaps incapable of seeing that we are invited to do the unthinkable: set aside our own comparatively small interests for the long-term survival and well-being of future generations and even the Earth herself. Like most of the CEOs of our biggest and most powerful corporations, the current leaders of the biggest and most powerful nations on earth are not prepared to become great. They would rather remain small, and their pettiness may be all it takes to give a good story a bad ending.

So, should we give up? Should we feel helpless? Should we focus on blame and become ever more cynical, or even succumb to guilt and shame? I don't think so. I think we should invoke the spirit of the poet Shelley, the healer Florence Nightingale, the scientist Marie Curie, the freedom fighter Albie Sachs, the pantheon of men and women who have stood up and fought for something bigger than themselves, and have taken command of our own future by getting involved.

When an idea finds its time, people and events will assemble to make it possible. The day at Embercombe when the spade lay forgotten in the grass and I was held by the deep magic of the land, I asked creation to bring me the people I needed to make this garden flower – a garden of exploration, questioning, listening, and inspiration. I am indebted to many who answered this call – Azul, Joey, Jenny, Maria, Tomek, Jolyon, Elizabeth, Rick, Michael, Emma, Nick, Dolly, Jonathan, Dianna, Nelson, David. Many others. Together with them I also received much kindness and friendship from the nearby village of Ashton. I didn't get off to a great start, however. One of the first events that I organised at Embercombe was a gathering of people from all over Europe: psychologists, academics, doctors, gardeners, builders, architects, consultants, and others less easily defined. I was pretty much on my own with almost eighty people coming for a ten-day conference, and since Pathways already had five tipis, it seemed the obvious accommodation choice. I then found another eleven tipis and arranged catering, two mobile shower blocks, numerous toilets, and started trying to get one of the hangars equipped to provide a warm indoor space for so many people. The event was taking place in October and I had visions of frosty mornings, hazy sunlit days, and the deep rich scents of an English autumn. The tipis went up and the event took place. It started raining on the first day and it finished the following spring, or at least that's what it felt like. Halfway through the conference I was summoned to the phone to hear that there had been complaints about the tipis. Apparently all manner of rumours were flying around the village and many of the residents were not happy. I explained the situation and promised to remove the offending tipis as soon after the event as I could. Which I did, but it wasn't soon enough. Another phone call was delivered and I spent days in sheeting rain dismantling all of the tipis and then weeks trying to dry them.

In retrospect, I wish I had gone round, met people and explained the situation beforehand, but I was tired, hassled, and it had never occurred to me that these by-products of a previous corporate event could inspire so much fear. I had never realised how controversial and provocative tipis were. Quite a few neighbours made it clear that they considered the whole thing an absurd overreaction and I found two of them lodged in Embercombe's hedges trying to get a better view. Sadly, Mary is no longer with us – she was a staunch ally. Four years later, with perhaps one or two of the jury still undecided, we now enjoy belonging to the village and I could not wish for more helpful or generous neighbours. It feels important. If we can't build community in our own village, it doesn't bode too well for larger dreams. The village is important to me. I spend a lot of time away from home, often abroad, and often in challenging and intense situations. Returning to Embercombe and calling in at the village shop, talking over the hedge to John or bending Tony's ear for farming advice all give me a sense of place and belonging.

Embercombe is heart-stoppingly beautiful. In May, one or two heavy showers of rain followed by strong sunlight calls forth a rush of growing and fruiting. The land becomes deep green and pulses. The scents are exquisitely aromatic. The geese continue their endless quarrels, and the badgers execute their carefully planned assault on the vegetable garden. Buzzards wheel and circle amongst the clouds, and the deer move through the woods as silently as the bluebells uncurl and flower. The weight and intensity of such beauty is sometimes overwhelming. Creation is not a cartoon idyll, it is inconceivable power in motion, dreaming itself awake. As each new leaf unfolds another elfin voice joins the throng. Perfume wells from juices manufactured in arboreal laboratories. It is a month when love can be experienced directly as an infusion of sunlight and warm rain. It is a month when we are sometimes confronted with whatever is absent in ourselves. It can be a hard mirror.

As the summer months move by, energy runs strong in the fields of Embercombe. Vegetables are harvested and we go forward at full tilt. There is high excitement, the sound of children's voices playing, the throaty bellow of the tractor. Visitors come and go, helping with the work and sitting by fires at night as owls patrol the shadows. It is a place of conversations and a place of healing. Many who come are successful, ambitious, professional people, but they seek something or they wouldn't come. The physical work is important. It provides time for conversations to emerge naturally, and time for trust to grow. There is also a chemistry that takes place when people work hard physically. Somehow they become more available emotionally. With emotion comes something more real, more honest, more authentic, and this is when the more significant conversations occur. In some ways it's like the gorge task when I was at Limestone Manor, but much kinder. Time alone is important, as is time spent in quietness. Not doing, just being. Then – eating food that has been grown on this same soil, sharing the company of others who also search for meaning, reflecting and gaining new information.

Sometimes it is effortless, and sometimes each tiny step is hard won. Three summers ago the geese reared about seven youngsters. One of them was born slightly different from the others. He seemed to grow more slowly, and struggled to develop in the same way as his brothers and sisters. I think the parent geese delayed the departure day, hoping that he would catch up. Then one day the geese called to each other; there was an atmosphere of tension and expectancy. The wind was summoned to the water and the birds beat their wings. They took flight and, after circling the lake, flew south. On the shores of the lake, one goose was left. He had not succeeded in learning how to fly soon enough. For some weeks the family of geese would return each day and there would be a very joyful reunion. Then eventually they left and did not return. It was sad seeing this young goose alone by the water's edge, disconsolate and defeated by the challenge of flight. More weeks passed. Every now and then the goose would try to fly and fail. Roman, Azul's son, named him the Lonely Goose, and we all fell silent when we saw him so vulnerable. A few weeks later, the family returned, and when they rose to leave they had added one more to their number.

There have been a few lonely geese at Embercombe. Of the human kind. Life, they feel, has passed them by. Yet of course it's not life that ignores us, it is we who ignore life. We imagine that all we have to do is snap our fingers and indicate that we're ready for the next course. Disappointed, we lose ourselves in sadness, anger, cynicism, boredom, or we just become numb and retreat.

'What colour is snow?'

The question was spoken quietly, almost softly. A hand rested on my shoulder. I could feel the warmth through my shirt. I felt thin. As if everything was able to pass into me at this time, as if I could feel all of the pain, all of the beauty, all of everything.

'What colour is snow?' This time a slight insistence, a requirement for me to speak. I suspected a trick and was searching for the answer without applying myself to the question.

'What colour ... is ... snow?'

Something about snow touched deep and I found myself silently weeping. I could feel all the wonder of billions of individual snow flakes, the enormity of so much beauty lain at our feet year upon year and largely ignored.

'People just repeat beliefs. They don't look. Look now ... '

I looked closely – blues, purples, and getting closer still, all colours, flashing, sparkling, cascading into my eyes. If this is what it was to see snow for the first time, how much more was there that had been around me all my life and which I had never truly seen?

I stand before the wood. I feel its warm breath soft on my cheek. I know that I am seen. For a few minutes I allow myself to be washed in the rich textured sounds that spiral and unravel in all directions. I have come for a blessing. I need the physical touching with earth, with water. I draw the scents of the wood toward me, tasting. My feet are heavy, the weight of me upon the earth, reminding me of who I am. I sense I can feel movement beneath the layers of decomposing leaf mould, countless thousands of tiny roots probing in a darkness as profound as outer space. With sudden clarity I know I am observed by deer. I enter a deeper stillness. Not seen, but felt, touched gently with practised intuition. I allow a picture of myself quietly browsing on leaves and green shoots to take shape, gently, no rush. I breathe, relaxed, following rhythms that offer themselves available to all who care to listen. About my own business, quiet, present with the trees. The picture is sent with a soft breath and my unseen companion resumes her browsing. Colour abruptly fades as clouds salute the sun. The wood notices and the song of a small bird perched in the holly tree imperceptibly shifts in appreciation. Nothing is still, everything moves, and overwhelmingly there is a sense of water. Water in the air, in the earth, and water rising in columns hidden beneath the bark of the trees. Water in me, most of me – 70% water. Arrows of light plunge into the wood again, like the chaotic embrace of a long-awaited reunion. Shards of light break and splinter, revealing the sacred, and tears moisten my eyes.

I am ready.

I enter the wood.

Isle of Erraid Journal – 8

I slept through until 11.30 a.m. today. It's the first time I've slept in and it felt very good to have a long uninterrupted night. I put in a request to Charlie at Embercombe a couple of days after being here, asking for him to send up one of the electric blankets, and I fitted it a few days ago. What a difference!

The gales continue, but now the leaden skies have shifted to provide glimpses of a soft turquoise blue. Yesterday when I visited Balfour Bay the sea was a deep green as she came heaving into the bay. I spent some time thinking about friendship and friends. One friend wrote the prayer below.

TREE PRAYER BY ROCK STORM

Sacred Mother, Sacred Father. Most gentle teacher, Mother Earth
– Father Earth. Grandmothers and Grandfathers of the four Directions.
I ask you to come into my Circle and to hear my prayers. I share these
prayers with you as a statement of light for all those who would see. I
share these prayers as a questioning of the dark for all those who
would know.

I watch your Trees. I look to them in wondering. I look to them in the
questioning of my Life and my Challenges. I can see that they journey
through the seasons and they are happy and strong no matter what the
season. I can see that they accept the time in which they live and do not
try to return to the past nor to jump forward into the future. I watch
and I see that they do not resent where they have been born, that they
work with the gifts the soil gives them, with the Sun that is given them,

with the Moon that is given them, with the Rains and underground waters that are given to them, and with the air that is given them. I also see that, though they are given these great gifts and though they do not question the wisdom of the balance of the amount of these gifts, they never forget Who and What they are. The Fir never believes herself an Oak, nor does the Madrone believe she can be the Sequoia. I watch them swim when the great storms come to blow across the lands. I watch them reach out and grab the Wind to slow her down so that she will not tear the very skin of the Earth Mother. I watch them use that great Power of Wind and Storm to vibrate and then crack and shatter the stones within the Mother Earth so that more beings may eat and grow. I watch as they burn the hills with their 'Green Fire'. I watch as they combine all this great conjuring in order to bring fruit into the world. I watch as they trust. Trusting that the season will once again change. Trusting that they will continue their march to the Sea. Trusting that they will influence all those who will listen. Trusting that they will ever renew and never forget.

I ask you, oh great Medicines, that I may be a reflection of these Chiefs; no matter how small my Circle, that I may be a pure Mirror and reflect all of their parts equally. I ask you that I may know of their trust when I fear that things will never change. I ask you that I may be at Peace with the ground that my roots have found and yet, like them, that I strive ever for the Greatness of What I am. I ask you that I may see the Storms and difficult times in my Life as energy sources that I may utilise and share with the rest of my Sisters and Brothers.

I ask that when I am dry there will be Rain.

I ask that when I need light there will be Sun.

I ask that when I need support my roots will find Earth.

I ask that when I need magic there will be the Night and the Moon.

And I ask, Oh Great Ones, that I and all of my People can know these things so that we too may share our fruit with our Sisters and Brothers. Now I have painted my prayers in Light, the words have been written in the yielding Darkness. I am the Human. I am the Sun Arrow ... A'hey ah, I have spoken. Genan nach Uman Daowin!

CHAPTER SIX

Leaders and followers

The recognition that a profound change of perception and thinking is needed if we are to survive has not yet reached most of our corporate leaders ... nor the administrators and professors of our large universities. – Fritjof Capra

The same urgent need shrieks in the ears of us all. Because corporations are now so incomprehensibly powerful, and because the leaders of these same institutions have been the subject of my work this last twenty years, I have found myself imagining that it is corporations and their leaders who most need to change. It is not. As a friend said to me recently, 'Everybody who has a pension plan is a part of the same system'. As consumers we make choices concerning where to spend our money, and most of us spend it using criteria that have nothing to do with values or principles beyond our own self-interest. It is becoming more and more widely known that cotton and its manufacture exact a huge price upon the environment. Yet how many of us avoid buying cotton or seek alternatives? We know that every trip we make in our car, every flight, every electrical household utility, generates more CO_2, yet how many of us are significantly adjusting our behaviour in acknowledgement of our responsibility? We are so used to clichés that describe our own species as 'intelligent', we ignore the evidence to the contrary.

A sign of our times, a sign that poignantly describes the attitudes and preferences of our times, is the taste we have for the superficial. It is reflected in our politics, in our leisure pursuits, in our homes, and even in the life-goals we strive for. It is reflected in much that fills our time at work, even the products or services that provide the raison d'être for that work. Yet I don't recollect ever having participated in a conversation when those I worked with deliberately chose to set aside all hope of doing something meaningful. It seems we have arrived here in the same way that driftwood finds its way down the river, and finally beaches on some alien shore. It is the way of flotsam and jetsam. Of course we don't name this preference as it is, we are more subtle, and, to make it acceptable to ourselves, we package the superficial in something that is neat, well presented, confident and, ultimately, once again superficial. It's not that our work is essentially meaningless, but rather the way we allow it to assume a meaning that is disproportionate to the core truth it contains. To do this ultimately precludes other richer dimensions of experience because the questions cease and all time is used up – vacuumed to feed a dream not big enough to support a life and justify the time dedicated to it. In this way too, we develop and train our leaders.

There is a crisis of leadership and it is with us now. No matter where you look or which side of the political divide you sit, no matter whether we consider this issue from the perspective of corporations or governments, our leaders are failing us. And yet we fail them also. We get the leaders we deserve. If we are selfish, petty and self-serving, how can we expect them to be any different? If we sling our vote primarily on the basis of tax cuts and our personal convenience, why would most politicians be any different? If we insist upon fixing our eyes firmly on the ground and ignore the existence of an escalating social and environmental crisis of global dimensions, then we can maintain the pretence right up until the wave engulfs us. Then the debate will be lost in a futile scramble for the lifeboat. Out of the comfort zone and fighting for survival in the panic zone. Leadership is arriving at a time and place deep in ourselves and deciding to have an effect in our world. It is available to us all – at a price. We are at a time when we all need to find our own self-leader. It is possible to have an entire team composed of leaders, or a community of leaders, an organisation of leaders – it only means that they each have discovered who they are and what they have to give. Giving is active, not passive. It is the behaviour of leaders.

After all the millions spent on leadership programmes over the last two decades we still have to search hard for exceptional, visionary leadership. A few months ago I worked with the board of directors from one of our leading high-street corporations. As we sat at dinner supping fine wines and commenting critically on the service, I was asked what I thought the future held. Conversation dried, and around the table heads turned in my direction. It was one of those moments when we feel the uncomfortable presence of our own authentic Self leaning close to hear and record the reply. I knew for sure that the question was asked in the same spirit as one might hail a colleague as she passes by in the corridor: 'Hi, how you doing?' The reply is unnecessary and taken for granted. We don't even pause. We've already moved on. Quietly, privately cursing the daemon that sat on my shoulder so attentively, I commented that I perceived us to be in the centre of a crisis so huge and so profound that the future required of us, at this time, to engage conversations that for the most part we have avoided and even derided – conversations that plunge our thinking and our deepest longings to questions that mostly now live only within the domain of artists and poets. Questions of meaning, purpose, fulfilment, destiny and love.

There was a silence, punctuated by a few sage noddings of heads and blank stares. In that silence there lived a whole world of possibility, and it ended when the MD took it upon himself to put people at their ease with words that sought to offend no-one, said nothing, sought humour, failed, and left us bereft with only a sharp word to the waitress to bring us safely back to the small world of our choosing. Shortly afterwards, with those moments now flung aside and forgotten, I drew the sliding doors ajar and slipped out into the fierce cold of a January night. The stars blazed and the leaves crunched beneath my feet as I stepped down to the lake that shimmered metallic in the pale reflected moonlight. It felt comforting to be by the water looking out to the forest. I found myself embraced by the sky, by the trees that stood immobile, dreaming, drawn with charcoal, stark, wild, witnesses to the passage of untold seasons. Fiona would not have completed that silence by shuffling past it in this way. Life and death is what Fiona wished to speak about when we sat together by the lake at Embercombe, but then she was dying. And now, months later, as leaves unfold and birdsong again fills the combe, it is her ashes that whisper to the wind, for she has gone and we will not see her again. Just as dangerous as the cancer that voraciously consumed the living tissue of her body, we participate and encourage the destruction of this Eden we so gracelessly inherited. Must we wait until death becomes inevitable before we as leaders engage conversations on how to live?

In the world of corporate management development we have been coaching and developing leaders for years now, and most of it has served only to block changes that now are thrust upon us. How many of all those engaged in the work of leadership development truly believe that we are engaging questions that have the capacity to transform, renew and inspire? And if our response is a swift reassertion of our spectacular difference, how much of our response is lodged with the need at least to believe that we are doing something worthwhile – a defence against self-criticism?

Much that passes for leadership in our organisations could better be described in the language of obedience and conformity. Real vision cannot embrace conformity, yet most organisations, indeed our very society, insist upon it, and just in case there is some doubt on this issue, we reward our leaders when they conform and punish them where they stray. At one point in my teens my mother found me a holiday job working on a pig farm. On my first morning I was initiated into modern-day farming. Marching hopefully behind the shambling form of my mentor, we walked down a broad shelving roadway into an underground hall. As the sheet metal doors swung open we were engulfed in the stench and raucous screeching of several thousand pigs. Penetrating the deep gloom we threaded our way amongst them, my companion lashing out with fists and boot, as if a dark hatred had lodged somewhere in his gut and only found relief in his role as gaoler. I thought we were going to fix a gate. Not so. We found one of the pigs lying on its side, listless and bleeding. Wordlessly I was motioned to hold its head between my knees. Then a hammer swung upwards and I watched as he shattered the skull and beat the creature's brains to a pulp. I couldn't speak. I stared at the flecks of blood that sat like red tears, bathing the hands that had held the pig still. The hands of a youth who was working here on this farm because he liked animals. My hands. I felt engulfed in horror, sadness and self-disgust. Later I learnt that when pigs are kept in these conditions they begin to exhibit the same kind of behaviour witnessed sometimes in humans. Any pig that develops in some way different from the others, bigger or smaller, is then singled out and punished by its companions. Once begun, at best this leads to persistent persecution. Quite often it results in death. When pigs are kept in the conditions for which life created them, when they are outdoors, able to root about, explore, and form relationships, when they can do what pigs love best and experience life, they do not develop the anguished delinquent behaviour of the concentration camp internee. Neither do we. Yet as leaders we cage ourselves and others into prisons that will, given time, expunge all true connection with life, with earth, with our own authentic self. If we are to be leaders then we have to meet the challenge of our own institutions – the same institutions that rapidly engulf what remains of our forests and what remains of our own wild nature. The same institutions that exist solely for the purpose of making profits and gaining power, and which so ruthlessly use up the lives of those who work for them or live through the spun dreams they hold up as a promised future happiness.

Conformity has no place in leadership. It is the place of the slave.

Conformity is a big and awesome challenge to the emerging and current leaders of any society. Yet how do we see ourselves for what we are? It hurts to see ourselves as slaves, so we dig deep into denial, and scour any source to refute what stares us in the face. The monster that rattles the cage of our Western culture is our acceptance of a system that values property and money above life. It is as stark as that. We do not have to live this way. Profit is the means towards something. It is not an end in itself. Profit is the vigorous, optimistic output of disciplined entrepreneurial activity, and the means by which we fuel greater causes of true meaning. Profit is a power. It requires wisdom to direct it.

Instead we place our would-be innovative leaders in offices that are, mostly, dreary conformist buildings in which it is hard to tell whether the sun is shining or not, what country you are in, or anything distinctive and challenging to the status quo. Occasionally we see the desperate attempts of people to assert their right to individuality by decorating their desk, customising the desk-top on their computer, or sporting a colourful tie. It is all that remains to us. And when we send our managers out travelling, we book them into hotels that look remarkably like a buffed version of the office – a place in which we measure value by the absolute predictability of everything that occurs, and the guarantee that they will never know anything real of the people or land they visit. We call this particular form of predictability 'quality'. Loneliness is a better term.

There is a long-term, ongoing, invisible training process that persistently encourages us to think along pre-set avenues and in pre-set ways to pre-ordained conclusions. We are persuaded to drop our childish dreams of longed-for fulfilment. Ideals are torn from their nesting-place and thrown to the wind, and the wind scoops them up and holds them close until perhaps one day we reclaim what was always ours. The only thing that is ours – the knowledge that we have a destiny, something of importance to engage with, to converse with, to be with, in life.

Creativity is the victim of conformity. It is crushed and ridiculed, becoming a gene, the prerogative of 'professionals'. Without creativity and the freedom it hungers for, we are already dying and everything we touch will carry the odour of decay. If we want leaders who are rolling back the limits of what is possible, then it requires a strategy every bit as dramatic and effective as the relentless gravitational pull of conformist thinking.

Leaders need to be dangerous to the status quo, and restless truth-seekers. They exist to articulate the dreams and aspirations of a community and then strive to gather the people's collective power by providing inspiration and continually proving their dedication and service. Leaders need to be seekers. They get burnt but they don't give up. They return. Leaders must be accountable. They must sit with the people, side by side as equals, and listen. Leaders without ideals, without principles, without vision, without...

Leaders are not led by the nose, they do not serve the needs of today at the expense of tomorrow. And they care for the children. They do not talk of accountability while poisoning the food we eat, the air we breathe, the water we drink. We need to work towards a vision of leadership that begins with self-knowledge, respect for life, and a new concept of duty. It moves on stepping towards the big issues of our time, striving for balance, facing up to moral choices, inspiring, caring, coaching, and always remembering that work and life are not separate. Leaders are those whose actions, choices, compassion, energy, vision and resolution are recognised by others and who are granted the privilege of service to the community and to the land. A leader is anyone who in whatever capacity emboldens others to live their life with courage, hope, and integrity. Such leaders embody qualities that inspire others to their own journey of authenticity and service.

We need to remember who we are, and the trust placed in our hands.

We need to remember that when the time comes for us to die it may matter to us – it may be important, that we can look back along the trail of our actions and feel proud of who we are and what we have done.

Leaders are born when two core changes, central to our identity and development as humans, take place.

In some way, in some form, sometimes looked for, sometimes unbidden, we experience the authentic and become true to ourselves, uncluttered with the accumulation of borrowed values, attitudes and pretence. We become aware of the difference that sets our old self apart from the new, and with this awareness comes a sense of huge relief. What was previously so arduous now becomes almost effortless. Where anxiety and tension existed we now find mindfulness and a clear sense of purpose. Authenticity has tangible qualities. It is visceral, and known immediately when met.

Authenticity opens the way for inspiration, or perhaps it sometimes happens the other way round. Inspiration is possible when an individual finds true relationship with life, and the vast potential that sits waiting within each one of us. Inspiration crackles like fire and is massively contagious. It can even dissolve the conformity of practised cynicism. Inspiration is energy. It is uplifting and a close relative with laughter, tears, and joyfulness. Where inspiration meets authenticity, we have leaders who will recognise the needs of the time, point the way, empower all they meet, and take action – even if it means considerable personal sacrifice. Even so. In fact, let's go further: it *will* involve personal sacrifice. True leadership always does. It goes with the job. If this is enough to dissuade us from leadership, we are not yet ready. We remain a taker, an exploiter, a fool who believes that by accumulating money and power we will become in some way a companion to the gods. There is no fulfilment without service to others.

An inspired leader, who speaks and acts authentically as her or himself, is unstoppable because they know no other way, and the leadership they represent is self-evident in all they do.

As things are now, we are engaged in a war with ourselves, with life, and the lines are drawn. The environmental degradation of our planet continues apace, the World Bank records that the gap between the world's rich and poor continues to wrench apart. World population is set to double, the bio-systems of the Earth herself are now under serious threat, the oceans are dying, desertification hurries on, and fresh clean water becomes ever more scarce. Ignorance is no longer an excuse. The consequences of warring against ourselves and winning are terrifying. We hack and thrust at our Earth, gouging lesions that weep and spill. We appear so crazed in our lust for blood that we no longer have ears to hear or eyes to see that it is our mother we harm so terribly – our son, our daughter. Mummy, Daddy, what did you do in the war... ?

It is now with the people. It is with us. We are called to become leaders. No matter that you and I both feel woefully unprepared. It doesn't matter. We have to get involved. Business could become the power that heals, but we can't wait to find out. I have worked with hundreds, actually thousands, of business leaders and I have enormous respect for their skills. If – when – as – increasing numbers of us collectively challenge the stranglehold that shareholders have on company profits and redefine the purpose of organisations, business may yet receive the laurel wreath. But even as increasing numbers of people call for change, we, as individuals, can't wait to find out. Maybe long ago, snug beneath your duvet, you childishly imagined that you were called to defend your people and perform deeds of great valour. It's not a dream. You have been called. You are on notice. The time is now, and it's not childish, and the duvet is about to be ripped away. If the body is willing but the mind demands to know under whose flag you are called to stand, then let the answer be the children, or the meadows in which you have made love, or if all else fails, your pride. History is peopled by many women and men who found their calling and courage the day the storm clouds gathered and the enemy seemed strong beyond imagining. As Gandalf said to Frodo:

> 'All you have to do, is decide how you will use the time that you've been given.'

Isle of Erraid Journal – 9

The wind has shifted to the south. It is blustery and sunlight dances amongst the crags and ancient deserted fields now left to the care of wind and rain. I climbed a steep gully filled with moss-covered boulders and entered one of my favourite glens. Standing there, taking in the soft warm air, watching the clouds curl in over Cnoc Mor, I heard a loud penetrating croak. Flying in from the east a Raven came straight towards me, snapping its wings closed and flipping on to its back, then opening the wings and reversing her rotation, again and again. Moving from one side of the tiny valley to another, craning to look at me, landing on a rock outcrop just forty feet above and peering down, she kept up the most complex array of sounds, and when flying demonstrated a whole array of flight manoeuvres. Mostly they looked unnecessary, hundreds of flips, glides, deliberate stalls, swoops and all the time calling, calling. I had the strongest sense possible of her well-being, her intelligence, curiosity, and her exuberance. This went on for almost ten minutes. When I thought she'd finished, back she came again. So I called up to her. She circled above watching, even landing again, the better to observe and listen. There was an amused interest on both sides.

The wind picked up and a shadow darted in amongst the sunlight. I looked up again and the Raven had gone, silent, as if absorbed back into the invisible. In the Earth Wisdom teachings of the Americas, the Raven is the Teacher of Natural Law. I had the feeling I had just received a tutorial. So I ask, what do I see, what do I feel, what do I sense … ?

I run the images backwards and look again. The Raven spoke to me about improvisation, spontaneity, experimentation, having a go, and not worrying about making mistakes. The Raven said:

'Get out there. Fly, travel. Say what you have to say, but don't forget to have fun. We're with you. We fly by your side. You will not be alone.'

Sunset over Cnoc Mor, Erraid

When Embercombe's lake was constructed, many years prior to my arrival, it was controversial and caused a lot of bad feeling in the village. The way it was done made the tipi fiasco seem subtle in comparison. The great gash in the ground was taken in hand by the combe and every year she becomes more beautiful still. I had a visitor last summer who stood, hands on hips, glaring at the lake. I'm not used to people looking at the lake in this way and so I also turned my gaze to the water and tried to see what he saw. It didn't work, what I saw pleased me greatly. There are some ornamental trees and shrubs planted nearby but mostly the lake is fringed by rushes, ferns, willow, birch, ash, oak and beech. There are irises, orchids, tall delicate grasses, Fleabane, St John's Wort, violets, buttercups, primroses, foxgloves and countless other wildflowers. The water has a reddish tinge and it smells gorgeously fresh. Throughout the summer months swallows swoop and glide taking the insects that abound, and thousands of little frogs march from its shores each year.

'I don't like artificial lakes,' he said.

I like this lake. I like it so much that I decided that I'd like to sleep near her for a while. I wanted to feel closer, more intimate with all the other creatures and beings with whom I share this bowl of hillside water. It's not enough to love at a distance. I need physical proximity — to touch, smell, taste, see, and hold close.

Early morning. I open the stove and place small pieces of tinder on glowing charcoal. Tiny pulses of smoke levitate and wander. Crouching by the wood stove I allow the night to linger in my memories of dreams fleetingly remembered. It is a vulnerable time, a time of hope and doubt, a time of reflection and anticipated action. There is an impulse to begin this new day, and a secret, guilty desire to stay where I am, listening. Looking out of the window I watch the south-westerly breeze chase unseen corridors across the lake, and feel the boat tilt under me as she joins the dance. Still visible, the moon seems to be travelling from west to east until I realise that it's the boat that's revolving on the mooring buoy. The sun glides across the field like water from a burst dam, seeking, probing, unstoppable. Each blade of grass is touched, blessed by light. The meadow is sodden with water. Like a great sponge filled to capacity, it exudes a kind of taut expectancy. The sun is welcome. My mood shifts. It is as if, like one of the blades of grass in the field, I am touched by sunlight and invited back into action. Hurrying now, I pull my clothes on, eager to be with the day.

The boat is tiny, a kind of floating pontoon with just one room sixteen feet by seven. At one end, to one side, is a small squat wood stove flanked by three steps rising to the cabin doors. Opposite the doors, at the other end, a bed squeezes itself

On board *Leaf* at Embercombe

into the confined space, pleasingly illuminated by three windows. A desk that folds up to the wall, a chair, and a small cupboard with a gas-ring stationed above. This is the boat I have named *Leaf*. Towards the end of the day, when it comes time, I leave the house and walk out into the dark mystery of the night. The path coils across the land, revealing herself as I move towards well-known landmarks, the looming outline of the whitebeam tree, the bridge, the bramble that each night I swerve to avoid and mentally note to trim, the grass path that contours around the lake, and then the woodpile stacked and immensely satisfying in its promise of future warmth. *Leaf* was an inspiration. The lake beckoned. After many years living on a narrowboat, I missed the closeness to the elements. I had grown used to living with the sounds of the season, geese announcing their arrival, the incessant chatter and laughter of ducks, the songbirds and the intimate profound scent of earth, trees and grass. When the idea first landed I didn't pause to weigh the practicalities but immediately started making arrangements. *Leaf* was in London, neglected and suffering. She had to be towed to the marina, lifted out by crane, pressure-hosed and painted. The crane was hired again to lift her onto a lorry, and the lorry made its long and ponderous journey to Devon. Then another crane. This time lifting *Leaf* from the lorry, over a hedge, and onto a farm trailer. Finally, at the lakeside, illuminated by the headlights of two tractors, she was pushed off the trailer and into the lake. For a few seconds we all held our breath as she lurched from side to side, threatening to overturn. Then, curious to inspect her new home, she slid into the darkness and disappeared. When later I idly calculated the cost, it considerably exceeded her notional value, but not to me. The lake beckoned.

At night the oil lamp glows and pulses in the shadowed alcove holding favourite books. Flames flicker and dance behind the sooted glass of the wood stove, and the wind rocks *Leaf*, spinning her around the buoy, as a mother might push a child's swing. Night after night throughout one wintertime, I was bathed in the starlight of Orion so generously suffusing my sleep and dreams.

The Invisible Path is always with us – whether we acknowledge its existence or not. It takes no offence at our indifference. However, when we recognise it, our attention and intention unlock previously inaccessible reservoirs of energy. It is a revelation and, once seen, nothing is ever quite the same. Joy is forever deepened and misfortune set in context. Life is challenge, but challenge is not to be feared. Everything has to meet the exigencies of becoming. This is the path of growing. When becoming is understood as the miracle that it is, we cannot remain sad for long.

There is too much of the new and wonderful to remain stuck nursing an old wound. When we invite the magical into our world she is only too happy to oblige. The young of all creatures teaches us this. Curiosity, playfulness and humour can take us a long, long way. New encounters with people, with plants, with animals, with places, with thoughts, with feelings – all assume a significance that polishes our journey along the shining way.

In 1996 Pathways was running one of the modules for Hongkong and Shanghai Banking Corporation's graduate programme. Bricket Hall was HSBC's training campus and, like most similar places, failed spectacularly to project an image of innovation and the adventure of new horizons. Stolid, complacent and depressing would be adjectives that more readily jump to mind, and for this reason I was not as tuned to the possibility of synchronicity as I might otherwise have been. However, in this particular group of HSBC graduates there were three young men from Eastern Europe whose company I particularly enjoyed. One of the Poles asked if he could put a friend of his in touch with me. She was confused about her future direction and he thought she might be well suited to Pathways. I often had conversations like this and, even though we swapped contact details, I didn't think any more about it. A few days later the phone rang and I listened to one of the most enthusiastic, positive, humorous and energetic personalities I'd heard in a long time. Her name was Dorota Ostoja Zawadska and she wanted to start Pathways in Poland. Poland would be Eldorado for Pathways. Pathways was a wonderful company, and Poland needed Pathways. This was the rough gist. The phone call was a welcome respite and I could have chatted for hours with this woman but it all seemed just a step too fanciful. She was twenty-four sounding like eighteen, had never worked, knew nothing about business and certainly nothing about organisation development. She'd been chilling out and climbing rocks for the last year or so, and ... It was enough. I finished the call with:

'Look, if you're ever in the UK give me a call and let's meet up.'

It sounded lame, but I felt we had run out of juice and there was nowhere left to go. Not so Dorota Ostoja Zawadska. She put the phone down and got on a bus. Two days later she rolled into Victoria Bus Station in London and called me again. We did meet up and it was just as impossible as it had been on the phone. During the early Limestone Manor days it was conceivable for a complete novice to step straight into the management development world and make a success of it. Most of the training used at that time was so unbelievably boring that any form of experience-based methods made a pleasant change, but in 1997 things were a lot different. Not only this, but bringing Pathways through the recession had left several of us very unwilling to enter another period of financial risk. Investing in Poland on the basis of one very personable young woman did not seem a sufficiently robust argument in favour of the project. However, even at that early stage it was quite evident that Dorota had bucketloads of charisma and a charm that was as unique as it was irresistible. I decided to look for a programme that we could invite her on and then see how she did.

We were working with the Ecclesiastical Insurance Group at the time and an opportunity came along. For some reason this particular course was extremely emotionally charged and our team were hard-pressed dealing with the fear, anger and suspicion that kept bubbling to the surface. Dorota witnessed all this and became even more enthralled. Anxious to make an impression she focused on being noticed and made a number of spectacularly inappropriate interventions. It was not looking good and she knew it. I was again subjected to intense lobbying for a second chance and although I felt it was all doomed to a sad and disappointing conclusion, I found one. We went to Snowdonia and back to the gorge. It was freezing cold and this time a rather more subdued Dorota focused on being helpful. She took this to extremes and I remember looking round to see her positioned half-immersed under a cascade of water as she assisted the participants over a tricky stretch. She was, quite literally, blue with cold. I knew that I was meant to witness this and although I felt exasperated at her tactics I couldn't help admiring her determination. Then she blotted her copybook again by staying up all night with the delegates dancing, drinking and flirting. Although I knew she would become a friend, we were fast approaching the end. I tried to kill the idea of Pathways in Poland by telling her that we simply couldn't do it, so she went back to Poland and with the help of her friend in HSBC drew up a business plan. I felt as if I was drowning. We studied the business plan and although I didn't believe any of it, I was beginning to think that we might, just might, make it on the strength of her fanatical dedication to the idea. We arrived at the moment of truth when I said:

'If you go back to Poland and fill a week with four appointments a day, with large well-known multinational companies, senior managers who have both a need and a budget, then I'll come over and we'll see what happens.'

She did it. From a standing start she pulled every string, exploited every contact no matter how remote, every waking hour, and, with no resources whatsoever, she did it. I asked Chris Walker, a friend and colleague from Limestone days, to come with me and we won work with J Walter Thompson, Reebok and Proctor & Gamble. Chris gave Pathways Poland everything he had and it made a big difference. It was very hard when I finally had to terminate his contract but it was self-evident that the business would not survive a UK consultant's salary and expenses. From then on it just got harder and harder. I had to pull out of most of my UK commitments and dedicate myself to trying to build another company. For all her commitment Dorota had a long self-development journey ahead of her, and as a young and attractive woman in the highly competitive and macho Polish business environment, it was a hard journey for her. Alcohol was a big challenge. It fuelled almost all training courses and made tough situations dangerous. Dorota assembled a team and fought for survival. I would fly in and work eighteen-hour days. We wrote hundreds of proposals and, in spite of the promising start, we lost money every month. By now my UK colleagues, having supported me in the first instance, were seriously questioning the whole thing. We pressed on and it still didn't work. Finally I flew over to tell Dorota and her inspirational team that it was all over and we could no longer subsidise her business. She was expecting it and listened quietly. Then she spoke, informing me that her team had waived their salaries and were burning on thin air. She asked for one more month and I couldn't say no.

That month they made a tiny profit.

I knew nothing about Poland before I met Dorota. I had a few confused and jumbled images of shipyards and grey overcast skies, all overlaid with the horror of the Nazi and Russian occupations. I now know a lot more. It is a great country, and the Poles are an indomitable people. I am very grateful to have had the honour of working there and of being befriended by so many warm and talented people.

Standing next to Dorota were two good friends, Bogdan and Ywona. Dorota has known Bogdan from childhood and he has stood by her through an endless chain of challenges that would have flattened and exhausted most. However, he was not able to help with the facilitation of the courses; for this she was totally dependent on Ywona. When Ywona died in a car accident it was tragic for all of us. She was a warm-hearted, passionate, and very gifted woman. She was a loyal friend, and she was a deeply special person. Her death nearly derailed Pathways Poland. Now Dorota had to dig deeper still and, while doing all I could to help, I watched and held my breath. It is impossible to name all those who rose to help our business through those dark and difficult times, but they were many and without them we could not have made it through.

Dear Friends

I am returning from Iwona's funeral. Many people were there, and it was as might be expected a very sad and deeply moving event.

The reason for my writing to you is, however, the overwhelmingly positive evidence that has been shown to all of the team here in Poland, of the caring and generous nature of our people – in Russia, in the UK, in Poland. As someone who has been in close contact with Dorota and her team these last few days I can say that I am truly proud of the spirit that has shown itself in so many ways - speaking a language of human care and consideration that has gone way beyond the polite requirements of professional colleagues.

I don't know whether you need to hear these words, but I needed to write them – so moving has been the individual and collective demonstration of kindness and love.

Iwona has left a young 13-year-old daughter – Agata. She is bright, talented, and has been very much loved by her mother. I am sure that she is suffering very deeply right now, but I am glad to say that though she is young she is also resourceful and resolute. It seems that she will live with her father and that she very much wants to retain and continue a relationship with Poland's Pathways team, particularly her mother's friend, Dorota. Financially she will be okay, and having only met her twice I still feel confident in saying that this young woman will find her way.

The flowers that were sent by each Pathways company were abundant, fragrant, and in all ways beautiful. The grave was a mound of flowers and the May sunshine splashed and slanted across the several hundred gathered to say goodbye and comfort each other. All around Life reminded us of her beauty and the power of friends to remember and honour each other. I am thankful that I am a part of a community of people who so fully respect each other. The letters, the emails, the phone calls, the faxes – I wonder if you know how many were touched, not just by words of sympathy for Iwona, but for the warmth that your caring brought to bereaved friends devastated by the death of someone so close.

Lastly, you should know that there has been laughter also. Quite a few years ago now I had a dear friend, Stella, who died of cancer. Stella was many things, but amongst them she was certainly great fun. She pursued her joys with dedication and tireless energy. It seems Iwona was cast from the same mould. The stories of her innocent excesses, her idiosyncrasies, her paradoxes, and her earnest struggle to remain sophisticated at the same time, are little short of inspirational all on their own.

May our company always celebrate love, and warmth, and generosity, and humour, and caring - in the way so tragically revealed to us all these last few days.

Love, Mac

Eleanor, Stella, Iwona, Fiona, Elsa. All are dead and all were young. My father also, dying at an age similar to my own now. How do we make sense of these tragedies? I have never really understood why people find their faith challenged when a loved one dies. To die is not a punishment, it is a shifting of realities, a passing from physical form to spiritual essence. Those that die are not in mourning. Dying is the great adventure that awaits us all, and although I love my life passionately and will fight to keep it, I do not dread death. What I have feared is not living my life while I have it. In the last twenty years I have met many people afraid to live – people who give all their energy to trying to remain safe, secure, and without discomfort. To be left behind after a loved one dies – this is different, and it hurts and hurts, but this is our loneliness, our bereavement. In a sense it is selfish, and quite rightly too. The more profoundly we can meet and engage with life, understanding ourselves as forever a part of everything, the stronger and 'safer' we become. A flame that burns and finds expression for a while before drawing back to the source.

I first heard this poem spoken at Betty Stanbury's funeral in Ashton. I have heard it attributed to two different sources, but both involve a scribbled note found in a soldier's pocket:

Do not stand at my grave and weep;
I am not there. I do not sleep.
I am a thousand winds that blow.
I am the diamond glints on snow.
I am the Sunlight on ripened grain.
I am the gentle autumn rain.

When you awaken in the morning's hush
I am the swift uplifting rush

Of quiet birds in circled flight.
I am the soft stars that shine at night.
Do not stand at my grave and cry;
I am not there. I did not die.

Spiritual experience is what builds spiritual strength. Beliefs always tend to be hostile to other beliefs because, if theirs are right, what does that say about mine?

For something so absolute, so defiant and so incomprehensible, we give death scant attention, until we get older, of course. My father died when I was twenty-three and the most egotistically selfish and self-centred I've ever been. Inevitably I was deeply affected by his death, although my tears were mostly shed privately; on some level, however, I refused to allow the tragedy of his illness to penetrate my preoccupation with life as I wanted it to be. Intimacy is so precious and so easily left aside when the world shouts for your attention. Later, as I grew up, I was ashamed how little I gave of myself at that time, to him or to my mother, but that is what life gives us – the opportunity to experience, learn and change.

We talk of Iwona still, and a tree grows for her in a garden in Kashina, Dorota's parents home. I feel her now, a living force that reverberates and echoes, reminding me to kneel at the well and drink deep, breathing my thanks upon the cupped water sparkling in my hands.

Knowing Dorota and finding that I had met a life friend led me on to meeting her family. Her mother and father, Krystyna and Ryszard, welcomed me to their home countless times, and, sitting outside by fires under the stars, we have also become friends. I used to hear about Dorota's maternal grandmother, Maria, and the more I heard about her the more I wanted to meet her. So on one of my visits Dorota and I visited her apartment. Maria was in her early nineties when I first met her. When much younger she had owned thousands of hectares of land and the villages that were located within them, and she was remarkable for her wisdom. She had no affectations, and no interest in her aristocratic lineage. Speaking seven languages and captaining her own yacht as a young woman, she spent most of her time working on the land shoulder to shoulder with the other villagers. Fierce, proud, independent, a feminist, and razor-sharp, she was a formidable force even at ninety-two. She was a committed Catholic who also had no truck with ignorant or corrupt priests, and her undying passion and love was the land, earth. I once asked her who had taught her to love the land so deeply. She fixed me with her hawk eyes and remarked,

'The land, stupid!'

Maria and Dorota

We talked on about land and her voice took on a reverence and love that filled the room. Then she spoke of her land and I saw endless miles of forests and broad open spaces, but something jarred until I realised that she was talking about a place that she still possessed. So I asked if we could visit it, and this tiny, ancient woman took us down the stairs of her apartment and outside. We climbed over fences, descended steep embankments, and negotiated broken gates and rubbish until we came to her land. It was a few square feet of earth, no more than a small bedroom, and here she came every day with her dog and gardened. She was too old to stand, so she would sit, and the smallest job would take all day. I couldn't speak.

A year later and her health was failing. I wanted to give her a present – something that would really mean something. So I took her a small stone in a box on a nest of pine needles gathered from the forest. It was special to me and I'd had it for some time. She couldn't get to the garden any longer and it was breaking her heart. I was giving her the land. She took the little box and her old hands fumbled the lid open. I was worried that she might think it an odd gift, but I needn't have worried. She was completely overcome and her eyes filled with tears. She clutched the stone to her breast and bowed her head silently weeping. Dorota and I also.

'This is for my healing,' she said, and we cried more.

For the remainder of her days she carried this stone with her and told everyone who visited her that it was for her healing. The stone was to have been buried with Maria. Instead, on some intuitive hunch, Dorota's mother kept it. Krystyna works mostly with schizophrenics, but also girls suffering from acute eating disorders. One of the young women she was treating was moving closer and closer to death and Krystyna had all but given up hope. On an impulse she gave the young woman the stone and told her about its history and what it was: the land. The girl was deeply moved and took the stone, refusing to give it back, and began to get better.

To those of us healthy enough to be cynical such things may not matter, but to Maria and to this young woman it did. The land can heal. It can quieten, and it can bring us to a place of truth, because the garden does not lie to us. We see how death works when we garden – how it furnishes the living. We can see and experience the circle, and we bathe ourselves in the wonder of participating in creation. Perhaps most gardeners don't think about it, they just feel good when they come in tired and hungry, flushed and alive. Or maybe we experience the garden by walking, or swimming, or sailing or ... What is important is the physicality of being with earth, and though we may not think about it, it is far deeper and more remarkable than our prejudice will usually allow. In handling earth we handle the substance of our own bodies. We become familiar with ourselves.

Isle of Erraid Journal – 10

Without beginning or end the waves roll in towards the shore. Standing here with the salt water foaming around my boots I am witnessing eternity. Wave upon serried wave journeys to this shore and spreads itself upon the soft yielding sand that we may understand creation.

There is no ending.
There is no ceasing as the waves caress the rocky shore.
If I wished to learn of perseverance this is the place.
If I camped here on the headland my life long, I would not come close to comprehending time as the ocean knows time.
The waves upon the shore are my breaths.
They are the breaths of all things living, which is all things. They are our heartbeat.
They are everything.
All waters of the earth search for the sea and long to be joined.
Even our water goes the same way.
All of creation knows the waters intimately and knows that they are joined.
Except humans. For us there exists the challenge of remembering who we are, and to whom we owe our existence.
If I wish to deepen my understanding of presence, the sea will teach me.
If I seek to deepen in meditation, the sea will teach me this also.
The sea teaches of birth and death, of creation and cycles of becoming and ending.

Thor did well when he was tricked by Utgardhaloki and drank deep on the sconce-horn causing the very first ebb tide. Like a great pendulum the great life-drum took up the beat lest we should ever forget that She is alive.

We were in Zakopane for the day, and browsing the market stalls. A friend of mine, visiting from America, and experiencing Poland for the first time, wanted to make a gift to the land and to the people. It is a tradition and an ancient Way that goes back to a time when tourism did not exist, and 'scenery' had not yet been invented. We approached one stall laden with smoked sheep and cow cheese. The elderly woman that attended to us possessed a grace and a kindliness that spoke across the divide of language and culture. When our friend was leaving Poland he asked Dorota and me to take a blanket that he would give me when I was next in the US, to this woman, as a gift from him and as an honouring.

During the late morning of a November day, as soft rain drifted in from the Tatra Mountains, Dorota parked the car and we picked our way amongst the puddles to the entrance of Zakopane market. We looked down the length of stalls wondering whether we would remember the face of the grandmother we searched for. As I turned my gaze from one woman to the next all doubts evaporated. I knew her immediately, as did Dorota. There was a pause as I readied myself. The medicine blanket warm against my stomach, sheltered under my coat away from the rain and cold.

Turning to face the old woman we walked forward into our ceremony. The woman lifted her eyes. She seemed somehow sadder, the smile I recalled now absent, a memory. I had asked Dorota to begin by saying, 'Grandmother, this man would like to talk with you'. Dorota spoke and the woman's face became alert, guarded, waiting, uncertain. I began:

'Last March I came here with an American friend, a man who loves our Mother Earth. We bought some cheese from you and you were kind and generous in the giving of a gift and a smile. My friend remembered you. It was one of the moments that made his time in Poland special. When I was in America this summer he asked me to carry this blanket and bring it to you. It is a prayer to all the grandmothers of Poland, for all the rivers and forests, and all that is beautiful in the land of Poland. It is a gift for you. This blanket has travelled from across the Atlantic Ocean, to England, and from England here to Poland.'

I unfolded the blanket and with Dorota we held it before her so that she could see its beauty. All the time as I spoke and Dorota translated, I could feel the tension growing between us. Together with my voice and Dorota's following like an echo, there came a third voice. A younger woman in her middle years on the stall to our left began speaking, saying again and again:

'Auntie, you see, some people are good, some people remember – even so far, from America! Auntie! it is a beautiful blanket. Oh, what a beautiful blanket. This is a big thing!'

With three voices speaking, the different languages, tones and cadences, the colours of the market, and the emotion of the giving, I felt I was standing in a swirl of energy, a twisting, spiralling column of spirit.

On the stall to our right a young teenage girl watched and listened. Her eyes were wide with wonder and a gentle tinkling laughter.

The old woman herself was simply overwhelmed. I could see her trying to think of what to say, what might be appropriate. As it was she only just about managed 'Dzi?kuje – thank you', and then began hurriedly filling a bag with cheeses to give to me. I gestured that no gift was necessary and managed to get the bag before more cheeses were emptied into it. We left with smiles everywhere, all around. The old woman stunned, still speechless, yet dignified.

We turned and left, continuing to walk up through the market. The sun filtered through the last of the rain and the river sparkled silver. We looked at the stalls yet saw nothing, our eyes and hearts still full. Then quickly, we found our way back onto the main street to find a coffee, apple pie, and a chair to sit upon by a fire.

There is so much magic and beauty available to us throughout every day of every year, if we go looking for it. On another occasion I was travelling with Azul in Lebanon. We were there to heal something that had been broken, and as with all healing work giving was at its centre. Azul had made some very beautiful pure gold earrings and we were searching for an unusual trade that would take us inside Lebanon – to her heart. After many false trails we made a trade and with one thing following another we found our way to children who had lost their parents in the long and bitter civil war. We had to struggle with indifference, our own conservatism, with suspicion, and with feeling inadequate to the task. Eventually doors opened, and the gold of the earrings became energy in the form of money, which bought materials to help these children become educated. Far more than this. The energy that was created by the journey, the struggle, opening doors that had been previously padlocked and then rusted, and the smiles and small gestures of affection from children we barely knew – in all of this is the heat and core of healing.

All forms of growing follow a pattern of discernible stages. This is our rite of passage, our time of testing. We have been taught to separate and hold apart many things that in truth cannot and should not be separated. Over hundreds of years we have exalted rationalism while ignoring intuition, feelings and love. We have allowed feudalism to seep into our very blood so that now we find it acceptable that we should feast while millions starve and thirst. It's normal. Everything that warms and gladdens us we have now placed under threat, and this is everything that nature is. Every year across the developed world people fortunate enough to have the means, stream out of the cities to find beauty. They do not head for the most ugly and polluted centres of our civilisation, they unerringly travel to the sea, the mountains, lakes and woods, and where they exist, cities containing fine and inspirational architecture. Many times, of course, we then destroy the very beauty that brought us there in the first place, but our first instinct was true. It is a deep and profound longing in humans – to perceive and experience beauty, to feel that we belong to life and are not held apart.

The summer of 2002 marked a very special time for Pathways Poland. The business has stood fast in the face of many challenges and David Mann now wished to give them a chance to move into a bigger frame. Together with Dorota and her team we discussed what form this might take and looked at the possibility of purchasing a property in Krakow. The idea was that we would create a project that demonstrated many of the values and ideas that we expressed in our work with clients. Pathways Poland would have their offices in this building and then they would offer space rent-free for small start-up businesses to gain a foothold and begin trading. In addition we discussed the possibility of a café and the requirement for a large room which would house many of the events and projects that we were hatching at the time. There was a lot of excitement as we went through that wonderful and emotionally exhausting period. Possibilities and potentials were explored, debated, cast aside, exhumed, re-cast, and then shelved as others come forward. At the same time the size of the commitment and the responsibility were beginning to weigh heavily. One evening just prior to David and me returning to the UK, and after a rather depressing sweep of available and suitable properties in the Kazimierz district of Krakow, boats intruded back into the conversation. There is something about boats that seems to sweep away common sense, and the usual self-protective cautionary principles that good business people apply to new ideas. Azul had just completed an inspirational community project on the river Dart in Devon and rivers were very present in all our minds. Without much warning the Polish project suddenly leapt off the bank into the Wiswa, or Vistula river, and from there it took off. This is a summary of the project as we explored the idea in 2003.

The River Vistula (or Wiswa) has its source in the Tatra Mountains of Southern Poland. This river is one of Europe's great waterways and travels the entire length of Poland to Gdansk and the Baltic Sea in the north. Both Krakow and Warsaw are located on the banks of this river and yet it is almost completely ignored, heavily polluted, and mostly unappreciated. Unlike almost all the other great European rivers there is a marked absence of river traffic (commercial or leisure), limited leisure facilities, very few businesses, very few people, no life. With the river located close to the centre of Krakow, attractively situated, it clearly represents a huge opportunity for investment and sympathetic development – especially so as Krakow becomes increasingly popular. A few years ago a group of us stood on the river's banks and imagined how a project could be devised that efficiently and powerfully achieves a number of objectives close to our hearts:

* return the river back to full health in terms of water pollution, biodiversity, habitat, beauty – along its full length;
* promote, inspire, & establish a flourishing environmentally sensitive leisure industry along the river in Krakow (and eventually further afield): restaurants, boat hire, taxis, tours etc. This will also serve the purpose of promoting the care and restoration of Poland's natural environment;
* promote, inspire and establish an arts festival centred around the river, that will bring business, community, environment and art together in celebration;
* devise a way in which we can use this project to launch a Corporate Social Responsibility (CSR) initiative in Poland that will inspire, inform and support other businesses to make CSR a practical, tangible and living reality within their own organisations.

Like every other idea before it and after, then began the real journey as Dorota and her team, together with David and myself, began trying to make it a reality. The boat had to be found, purchased, and then sailed to Krakow. There would be the problems of undertaking and absorbing a massive shift to the Polish business since we are organisational consultants and not a shipping company. There were endless problems and challenges, but none was more complex, tortuous, and bureaucratically labyrinthine than the task of securing permission, dissolving opposition, and resolving countless logistical and political complications. Notwithstanding Mr Koersten. A delightful character, very much in the style of the ancient mariner, and complete with long flowing white beard, Mr Koersten proved to be a wily, skilled and dogmatic negotiator. In fact, some months later we were sitting disconsolately on the river bank at the German border, having already paid for the barge and Mr Koersten's services in taking the barge to Krakow. He was playing his last card. He refused to take the boat any further unless we paid a supplementary fee of several tens of thousands of euros, immediately, in view of the arduous conditions. What was depressing was the knowledge that this kind of bargaining would never finish until we had parted company for good. Since the barge is big (50 metres x 8 metres), ancient (1890) and idiosyncratic, not many Polish skippers seemed too keen to take on captaincy for the last thousand or so kilometres. Nevertheless, we reclaimed some pride by concluding the negotiation and relationship with Mr Koersten by saying 'no' once more and ordering him a taxi.

Alrina is finally in Krakow and her restoration is in progress. When Alrina opens in 2007, she will have a bistro cafe and conference facilities, and the Pathways Poland team will do all in their power to use the project to engage conversations that will call forth ideas and actions supporting the vision of a just and sustainable future.

CHAPTER SEVEN

Close encounters

We stood in the kitchen. A conversation was beginning and I sensed that we would be travelling in delicate territory. Lisa was the wife of an old friend. She was warm, generous, and riven with self-doubt. I could tell that she wanted to approach the topic of belief but was nervous of where this might take us. So was I. Lisa was a Catholic and her beliefs were important to her. I had no desire to see them weakened, but I could also tell that she doubted their veracity.

'So, Mac, what do the Red Indians believe?' The tone was jocular but brittle, and the question left me feeling depressed. This was going to take hours and go nowhere.

'Why Red Indians, Lisa?'

'Well, it's what you believe isn't it?'

'Er ... no. You see ... '

'But I thought you went to America and things?'

It wasn't going well.

'I don't think that belief comes into it really, Lisa. When I visit my friends in the States I don't go to learn about them, I go to find out about me.'

She poured me some coffee and we gazed out of the window, watching her small child torment the cat.

'It's a long way to go when you're already here, isn't it?' We exchanged smiles and I had another go. It's not easy speaking words that seem archaic and overly serious, but then I knew that I had to take the risk. So while the words were what they were, my tone was light, soft, conversational.

'I love our Earth and I love these islands where I was born. I love the experience of being alive and the challenges that life brings me. I love the adventure of seeking to know myself, and I love and care for beauty. When I garden I feel these things, in fact I think that this is why people garden. It is prayer, really. In the garden they understand what it is to participate in creation, to be human. When we garden we bathe in beauty. We are reminded of how death feeds the living, and we observe the alchemy of sun, rain, air and earth. Deep down these things are known to us all, but we've lost respect for the garden, and so we've lost a bit of ourselves, and we feel lonely.'

She went outside then and I watched as the cat was relieved of its child-minding duties and the mother and child went into the garden. The child was helping and the mother was crying, but there were no tears, just waves of loneliness. I watched as the sunlight played on her hair and her hands became tender in their task of caring. I watched as the child learnt about tools and made efforts not to stand on the young plants. As the minutes passed by the woman became stronger and her movements more easily decisive, and across her face spread a glow that softened the sorrow and eased the tension. When they came in refreshed and energised we returned to our conversation.

'I don't get it, Mac. You seem to be suggesting that the garden is holy?'

'It is holy'.

'I think the church calls that heresy!'

Pause. 'Tell me Lisa, if I had used a camcorder and filmed you while you were working just now, and if I had shut off the sound ... what would you *see*?'

We stared at each other and I could see that she was watching the video. I could see that she was observing the state of grace that had so easily embraced her. I could see that she witnessed herself being blessed. Between us there was some understanding. She passed me a basket of potatoes and I ran water into the sink, cleaning them for our evening meal.

It is hot. The sun describes her furnace dance and my spirit is forged by great clashing blades of golden heat. It is hot as I lay upon the wood shavings of the dance circle, the drum sings out the heartbeat of life and the singers' voices swell in rhythm and power. The air is still, yet amongst the trees green leaves of delicate design shiver and awaken my concentration. Now I understand, now I understand the gift of water. My hand reaches out and fingers dig deep into the damp earth at the foot of the cottonwood tree. Muscles bunch and squeeze. And the tree speaks to me. I feel her as a sister, and I sense her encouragement. I am thirsty. My throat feels swollen. My voice is husky, altered. Yet I have been thirsty all my life, and stretched out upon the earth, I have a knowing of this little tree's love. Just above me, tied to a small branch my salbutemol asthma inhaler swung lazily. Asthma had persisted since my teens. On a daily basis I had been using an inhaler for three and a half decades. I never intended it to be it so visible. This was changed when it was suggested to me that I had a lot to be very grateful for from this ugly little contraption – that it had cared for me, and that the scientists who had created it had done me a great service. Struck by this thought yet still uncertain and hesitant, the inhaler was brought to the tree and was honoured. At this time, miraculously after so many years, it was fast becoming redundant. After thirty-five years of constant use I had been the beneficiary of a healing ceremony that I never saw and which took place several thousand miles from my place in London. Without any appeal for belief, almost casually, I was told that they would work for my healing. They did, and I was, healed – within three weeks of their determination to help me.

The drum becomes more insistent. It enters me and meets my heart. The same song, the same since creation. The drum teaches me about my heart, reminding me that it has worked tirelessly these last fifty years, powerful, strong, requiring no command. To get up takes effort. I'm amazed how quickly I have lost strength. I walk out into full sun, glad to be upright and facing the tree. The singing begins again and as the lead singer's voice rings out I find myself renewed and energised. The other voices follow and I sense a swelling of emotion deep inside me. A gasp escapes my lips and the first tear is wrenched from my diminishing water reserves. Colour and sound enfold me as I run for the tree, lips pursed around the whistle and my ears are filled with the shrill piercing sound cutting the air and dividing it. Great sobs tear themselves free and for no reason except long practised habit I try again to stifle them and back away from feeling so much. It hurts to feel. Yet it hurts more to shut the door on life. Now moving backwards, feet shuffling the long trail back to my bower, eyes fixed as lances of prismatic light upon the shimmering tree. I see vapour all around her and for the first time understand how she has to fight to drink and live. Waves of emotion now engulf me and I'm lost to any sense of pretence. Whether I like it or not, I'm present with grief and joy, simultaneous. Water, the gift of water. I reach the bower and sink to the earth, knowing appreciation as I never have before. The tree is burned upon my mind and I know that I love her deeply. Images of her grandparents flit across my mind's eye, a great line of ancestors disappearing into great swamps as volcanoes explode and the atmosphere clings thickly. I see countless millions of trees working tirelessly over millions of years, giving me the air I now breathe. I see them, the ancient cousins, beckoning, calling, inviting the humans to life. Now I am only tears and all the world drowns.

Two nights ago, as the moon slipped away and the blue dawn encircled my camp a doe brought her fawn to me. There is such a feeling of honour when a wild creature chooses to do such a thing. She came as shadows come, silent as the night herself. Without warning I was aware of her – she entered my space. Then the shock as I became aware of the fawn, perfect, very beautiful, still dappled as the young ones are, watching her mother, innocent, curious, happy to be alive with food to eat. I wonder at how lightly she imprints herself upon this world – as if her spirit so new to this young body needs time to settle and take more solid form. She is only one step different from the sunlight that balances on the madron tree's leaves, a brushstroke of colour. The fawn copies the mother, turning over leaves, intent. She discovers some squirrel's stash of hidden acorns and contentment washes towards me as she munches this delicacy. The doe quivers alert, relaxes and turns to clean herself. The ears never cease to scan and interpret. Silently I send out my thanks for this healing and the doe with her fawn slip away amongst the tall reaching oaks.

It is time to dance again. My thirst has become more profound, but a stillness, a peace, a sense of pride that I am living the life I always dreamed of and thought impossible now accompanies my unsteady steps. Again the drum and again the singers, and the tree grows larger as I close the space. I am the wind, and I am the tree, I know my brothers the crows, and I walk with the flowers. Nothing will ever be the same. I have gone deeper. My mind stretches and creaks as I see myself just a few weeks earlier wearing a suit entering one of my clients' offices in London's financial district. I'm looking a bit different as I dance back from the tree, feet marking rhythm, hands lightly holding plumes marking the same pulse. A smile curves upon my unshaven cheek, and dried saliva . It is good to be alive, now, at this time. Twenty-five years ago I first read some of the speeches of Native American chiefs, women and men, and wondered at the grace, dignity and authority they held while speaking of our Mother Earth and of 'our relations'. It is not naïve or childish, it is factually and genetically true. If we find it embarrassing, perhaps this has more to do with our own infantile self-importance than the idea itself. The world we now live in is hugely complex and our capability to innovate extraordinary and awe-inspiring. What is absent is the spiritual knowing that we have a family and a tribe to which we belong. That we have a duty to life. That we are beholden to that which gave us life. That we should be deeply privileged to be alive here on earth, and that with this privilege comes responsibility. Such insights assist humans in making choices that acknowledge the delicate fragile beauty that has held us nourished all these thousands of years and to whom we owe everything.

'I have shaken hands with a great many friends, but there are some things I want to know which no one seems able to explain. I cannot understand how the government hands a man out to fight us, as it did General Miles, and then breaks his word. Such a government has something wrong about it ... I do not understand why nothing is done for my people. I have heard talk and talk, but nothing is done. Good words do not last long until they amount to something. Words do not pay for my dead people. They do not pay for my country, now overrun by white men. They do not protect my father's grave. They do not pay for my horses and cattle.

Good words do not give me back my children. Good words will not make good the promise of your war chief, General Miles. Good words will not give my people good health and stop them from dying. Good words will not get my people a home where they can live in peace and take care of themselves.

I am tired of talk that comes to nothing. It makes my heart sick when I remember all the good words and all the broken promises. There has been too much talking by men who had no right to talk. Too many misinterpretations have been made; to many misunderstandings have come up between the white men about the Indians ...

I only ask of the government to be treated as all other men are treated. If I cannot go to my own home, let me have a home in country where my people will not die so fast ...

I know that my race must change. We cannot hold our own with the white men as they are. We only ask an even chance to live as other men live. We ask to be recognised as men. We ask that the same law shall work alike on all men. If an Indian breaks the law, punish him by the law. If a white man breaks the law, punish him also.

Let me be a free man – free to travel, free to stop, free to work, free to trade where I choose, free to choose my own teachers, free to follow the religion of my fathers, free to think and talk and act for myself – and I will obey every law or submit to the penalty.'*

*Hin-mut-too-yah-lat-kekht, Young Joseph, Nez Perce chief, diplomat, warrior – speaking on 14 January 1879 in Washington DC, to a gathering of US cabinet members and congressmen.

I tried speaking some of the written oratory of great chiefs like Chief Joseph of the Nez Perce, Sitting Bull and others. It was an extraordinary experience. As I formed the words I also felt their power. Words such as these command respect. They have a dignity and a pride that asserts itself and quietens. I felt quite different when I spoke these words. I stood more upright, and I glimpsed the tragedy that had befallen these people. I glimpsed the tragedy that had befallen my people. It is extremely moving to witness great spiritual strength unbowed in defeat, and the comparison with their spiritually bankrupt victors, almost unbearable. It wasn't long before I realised that the words I was reading were my thoughts and sentiments, but I was struck by the embarrassment that would consume me if I ever spoke so intimately and naturally of things I considered beautiful using my own words. I couldn't find the courage to speak directly to life. I allowed my embarrassment to lead me to betraying my love for the trees and grasses, clouds and birds, cattle and sheep, all of my relations. I betrayed them and I betrayed myself.

It was the third day and I felt like a soft white plum that had been dropped from someone's pocket into the hottest desert of the world and had now lost all moisture. My voice was a croak, and while I felt fine when I woke, a few runs towards the tree and my strength would desert me. I was in love and at peace. The singers, working hard, pushed themselves to meet the challenge of the final day. When not dancing we lay still upon the ground conserving energy, dreaming and praying. It was early morning and I had work to do. I knew that it was time to take my courage in my hands and break cover. So as the tree rushed towards me and the ancient songs rose and fell against the sky I spoke with life and made my request.

Late afternoon the same day the dancers sat grouped in the shade. Nobody spoke. There was a stillness that none would have willingly broken. The air was brittle and hot. Each dancer sat with their own thoughts.

We were waiting for water.

Without food and water for three days, our senses were acute and subtle. Each tiny sound had a resonance and a place. A jug was raised and sunlight danced on the sides of tiny waves of water. Water leapt from the jug and curved towards glasses, tumbling, splashing, and tiny bubbles wandered upwards to burst briefly on the glittering surface. Quiet words were spoken and we rose to meet water as we never had before, truly appreciative, deeply touched, caressed by the care of those whose dedication had brought us this ceremony of love. And we drank, and water trickled down dry parched throats, and all of us met water for the first time and knew that she is sacred.

Dear Friend

You have only to remember one thing:

Your Time will come.

It will.

When pressed from all sides by difficulty, challenge, sadness, and loneliness it is difficult to have measure - difficult to remember that the clouds are there for a purpose, and that in good time the sunshine will pierce the greyness and bring colour back into our lives. You are a spiritual being, a being of power, and if you choose, in this life you will rediscover your self. Yes, this is possible for you. No doors are shut. The opportunities you crave are with you now, and the future is born with every choice and decision you make now, and now, and now ... Life will not desert you. She loves you. She has always loved you. Nothing can change this.

Your time will come. Use the gift of your present challenges to prepare you for that time. This is business. Invest now, and work with what you have. Tomorrow you will be stronger, and then perhaps it will be time - you must be ready.

Once upon a time I remember a young woman arrived at our place for her ceremony. She had made very little effort to prepare and seriously engage with the meaning of this time. It had been given to her too easily.

She did not value the gift. She had not yet learned of value. So her ceremony was okay, and yet deep down she was disappointed, and just a little ashamed. In fact, she had not valued her self enough to give to her self a beautiful and powerful ceremony. Yet she was not a bad person, or a failure - just young and invincible and not yet present with the knowing that life is precious and often very short.

Now this young woman is a few years older and many years wiser. A close friend has died - suddenly, BANG, DEAD, GONE ... and just as suddenly, value is more intimately understood. When this young woman finds her way to another ceremony she will not approach it as she did the last. Things that had little meaning before will be full of meaning now. Life teaches us if we let her.

We are all of us this same young woman, just as you are she. We have to learn these things through experience. There is no part of our lives, no minute of each day that is without value. So, my friend, use this time well - hard as it undoubtedly is - and sooner or later the cloud beings that you think of as so grim will reveal themselves and be beautiful to you. So beautiful, that you will not know whether you are walking in cloud or sunshine. It will make no difference. It is life, and it will be your time.

Love

Mac

On the largest of our meadows at Embercombe there is a stone circle. We call it the Magpie Wheel. The Magpie Wheel is no garden ornament. Permission had to be obtained from the elders, and so journeys were made, to Ireland amongst other places. Years of work went into making this circle a possibility, years more made it a reality. Our Magpie Wheel is very young. Because in substance it is 'just' a circle of stones, many will assume it cannot have significance and treat it like scenery, a curiosity; but the Magpie Wheel is the story of this book, and more, much more. There are words that we have elevated to a status unworthy of their meaning. 'Scenery' is one of those words. It pretends to be innocuous, hiding in a sham simplicity. 'Scenery' is something that pretends all the time. When we perceive the land as scenery we are offering our sword and furling the standard. We are defeated and crushed. We no longer belong. We are tourists and the land cannot speak to us. In our hearts, sometimes buried and padlocked, we have an instruction manual that can guide us through the awful sterility of scenery. The Invisible Path forever turns towards this place. We will sense its breath against our ear. We will be spoken to. To get closer, go to the ocean or to the mountain or to the tree or to your own hearth fire, and speak to life directly, personally, and above all, honestly, of your longing. Then go about your day, but be alert.

In the summer of 2003 an Elvin piper came and stood by the wheel. Facing the north-west his pipes drew breath and spoke to the far-off Hoop of Gold. Standing nearby I felt that I could see the music tear at the distance and levitate a bridge between the visible and the invisible. The sound awoken in the pipes was old, raw, splintered and hoarse. There was the rising cadence of all such pipes as the sound was lifted to the sky and born on wings west across the sea. It was enough. The eye of the Dragon was open.

The stone wheel of Embercombe was brought to our land by two people with whom I no longer speak, our friendship shattered and set aside. Over many years I had studied with them, learning and experiencing things that I had hardly dared to

Winter sunrise on the Magpie Wheel, Embercombe

believe could one day be mine. Doors were opened, and I walked through them. During one ceremony I was invited to make a vow. This vow was to be made between me and life. In no sense did it imply any commitment to anyone else. Neither did it mean that I had joined anything. It was a promise to myself, witnessed by friends and guides. Vows are not very fashionable any more. They seem archaic and not of this world. When I emerged from the ceremonial lodge, sweat pouring from me in tiny rivulets, and clasped the arms that reached out to steady me; when I stood with my bare feet planted on the earth, and like the elvin pipes spoke aloud to the night sky, I meant every word. Years later this vow was renewed and the meaning sunk deeper still. It never occurred to me that in making this vow I would find myself obliged to stand against some of the people that had invited me to make it in the first place – my friends. But that is the Invisible Path, and that is the wisdom of the higher self that guides us on our journeys. Turning a corner I found myself confronted with information that drew aside a curtain on actions that were as sickening as they were true. To remain true to that vow I had to burn a bridge.

For some time those of us who care for this Magpie Wheel found ourselves suddenly bereft and uncertain. It was as if the circle of stones, speaking so eloquently of our earth, the stars, the moon, our relatives, you, me, the children, our world and universe, was tainted. This is not how we now feel. The betrayal of these stones is a matter of concern for many, but there are no teachers more important than the truth they teach. I am still deeply grateful for the generosity and wisdom that brought us the Magpie Wheel, personally grateful, but it is cause for celebration when the student truly understands that more important than the teacher is the guidance and counsel of his/her own integrity. As someone who has unwisely crossed many boundaries, I am very glad that I seem to have learnt to trust myself. I walk the Invisible Path without holding the hand of some revered human or human-created authority. These things can take so long to learn.

I have a niece called Eleanor. I say 'I have' because this is how I feel, but she recently died aged twenty. Eleanor was born with a condition known as arthrogryposis. It is a form of arthritis and in the more acute cases the child endures severely restricted movement in many, or most, joints. Eleanor spent her short life in a wheelchair. Although also partially brain-damaged she was bright, vibrantly alive, and had the most wonderful sense of humour. Wherever she went and in whatever circles she moved, she brought people together and she made people smile. Eleanor and others like her should always hold a very special place in our hearts. They teach us about bravery, about appreciation, and they teach us about values. They ask us to stop moaning and complaining, and acting as if we were powerless and under-privileged. They confront us with our selfishness, yet they never judge us. Eleanor did not lead a sad life. If there was any sadness, it was for others who did not really understand. In fact there was no sadness around Eleanor, except now for the fact that she is gone. Micky and Annie, her parents, and Bryony her younger sister, were undoubtedly challenged. Undoubtedly they had to dig deep to meet the extra demands that were made upon them, but that is our purpose – to learn and grow. They were enriched by Eleanor, and by meeting the challenge of her disability they deepened as people. Eleanor was a gift.

There exist two places that carry her name and her memory. One of these is the corner of a Cornish meadow where she lies buried, made beautiful by trees and a bench where people can sit and be with their friend. Another is a smaller stone circle on the isle of Mona, now hidden by briars, embedded in the earth, and known only to a very few. In this place, many years ago now, prayers were made and the gift of Eleanor's life was honoured. It is within our power to make of our lives a gift to others, if that is our choice – just as Eleanor did.

Isle of Erraid Journal – 11

I wrote the paragraph below quite a while ago now, but today I was reminded by a newspaper article commenting on how plants open for spring earlier and earlier each year as global warming calls them to stand forward. Whatever is worrying in this phenomenon, I shall always be happy for my first sighting each year of this delicate and wondrous gift.

There is a treasure of rare beauty hidden as a jewel amongst the briars of early Spring. I came upon this gentle being as a young man and now, each year, I take joy in finding her again. Few have ever truly met her, and those that have remain silent, too awed to shout her name. You do not make her acquaintance by chance. You search for her, or hear her tiny huge voice - the sound of a single raindrop splashing playfully against the newly unfolded green hawthorn leaf. She invites you to smile. Look close and she is a ruby happily lost amongst less graceful friends. Look closer still and she belongs to the exotic *famiglia* of the coral reef, sister to the anemone, tentacles tasting the chill March wind and seeking the caress of tiny lips. She is delicate, dignified, a generous friend. She is powerful too, and has birthed many gifts for relations of ours, human and animal down many generations. She is a teacher, a healer also - speaking of renewal, awakening respect and care. She brings us the question: how much else is there that glows and pulses within our fumbling reach that we might spend a lifetime ignoring? She warms my heart. She is the flower of Hazel.

In the autumn of 2002 I was coming down the Thames in my narrowboat *Mallard*. *Mallard* was once a steam-powered working boat. With an iron-riveted hull and three-inch-thick elm planking on her bottom, *Mallard* has class. Now powered by a vintage Lister engine she has a distinctive bass throb, and a solidity and authenticity that is very appealing. It was a bright day and I was enjoying the warm sun on my face as we slowly made our way south. I received a phone call telling me of Eleanor's sudden death, and I was very upset. The contrast between the news I had received and the gentle beauty of the river as it meandered through the water meadows was too stark. On an impulse I pulled into Abingdon and bought some flowers, provisions, and a magazine *Boats for Sale*. Leaving the town behind me I found a quiet stretch and stopped the engine, allowing the boat to drift with the current. Then I made my farewells to Eleanor, sending her love, and laying the flowers in the water. As *Mallard* pulled away I watched the delicate, fragile beauty of those flowers and the river water lapping against them. I saw them disperse a little, paint splashes of colour reflected in the smooth, clear, viscous water. I saw how beauty in all its forms caresses the tired aching spirit when it struggles to swim against the current, gently nudging us to be with life and join the river on her long journey to the sea.

That evening I leafed through the magazine and began thinking about the sea. For years I had owned narrowboats. In fact this is how I survived in London. Moving in 1987 from a cottage in North Wales on Mona just ten minutes from a small intimate beach, to a first-floor flat in Holloway was tough. I managed fairly well until the summer and then I suffered. I missed a garden of some kind. I missed the solitude that was always available on the Mona beach. A year or two later, while outside London near Tring, I was walking along the Grand Union Canal with a friend. We came across a string of narrowboats with people clearly living in them. I took in the scene – the smell of wood smoke, the sound of a cello, a couple of children fishing nearby, and a woman chopping kindling on a wood block. People were standing around drinking mugs of tea and there was the companionable sound of laughter and conversation. I was smitten with a longing to join them. By this time everything I possessed had been invested in Pathways and I couldn't raise the finance. Once again it was a friend from amongst my business clients that helped me make this dream come true. Sitting in a café with Robert, he enquired how I was doing in my attempts to buy a boat. I told him that I'd had no luck as yet but that I was still on the case, and he offered to extend me the loan. It was a huge gift, not only for the generosity that prompted the offer, but because it enabled me to get started with boats and it made my time in London very special. Eventually I secured a mooring in Little Venice, with a garden, and just a short journey to Pathways' offices in the West End. Now, cruising the Thames and thinking about the sea, I began to contemplate a different adventure.

Everything that informs my work is funded by the knowledge that our health, across all four of the human powers, is derived from an intimate and deepening relationship with our earth. Step away from relationship, become inflated with a belief that sets us apart from earth, trees, sky, flowers, rivers and animals, and we eventually go crazy. We become maddened by the belief that we are separate from life and that whatever is around us is there to be exclusively used for our own selfish benefit. We go to any lengths to justify our hunger, and our hunger is huge. It is a hunger that can never be satisfied, because it tries to feed us with food that never satisfies. The rich man goes on and on trying to get richer because he can never have enough. Compared to the wealth of his friends his fortune may seem small, and in any case how much do you need to feel protected against all the uncertainties that life might one day offer? Underneath the compulsion that amasses wealth is a greater hunger, a hunger to possess – as if by possessing something I am myself miraculously endowed with other less tangible qualities like self-worth. With my purchasing power I imagine myself as powerful. And underneath all of this?

'I wish to feel connected, to be accepted and to belong.'

It is a hunger for love.

The sea is another gateway. Like the mountains it brings us into relationship with the wilderness. Even a mile or so offshore from an island as overpopulated as Britain, the wild takes you in her consuming embrace. In my guts I know that we need to re-acquaint ourselves with the wild, and that in so doing we will unwrap the cloying, distorted enchantment that makes us so deeply afraid. In my mind's eye I could see a boat of wood and iron plunging in turbulent seas, and a ring of faces peering from hooded oilies as the wind whips the tops off the encroaching waves. I could see the fierce burning delight of eyes beholding the watery, salted wild at first hand, directly. Some fear as well, no doubt, but fear is part of excitement, and, providing foolishness didn't find its way on board, we would find our way back to the comfort of home, strengthened and gladdened. Leaders of organisations and institutions, young people, women and men from every part of our safe, occluded world, could find their hearts once more and quicken as the wild stroked their dreams.

With a boat that sailed the seas I could reach out for the horizon and grasp it. Horizons beckon and repel. They remind us of maps yellowed with age and scrawled handwriting that shakily describes 'here be monsters'. There are always good reasons why today is not the right day to turn our backs on the familiar and probe the unknown. Yet once we take the time to witness the sun's steaming descent into the distant ocean we know we have to follow one day.

So as I leafed the magazine it was to sailing boats of character that I was drawn, and a photograph of just such a boat jumped out of the pages and fastened itself on my imagination. *Volharding* is a sea-going eighty foot Dutch sailing barge, twin-masted, iron hull, a kind of 19th-century lorry. She used to carry timber from Norway to Holland as well no doubt as many other cargoes of different descriptions. Trying desperately hard not to get too excited, and failing miserably, it dawned on me that *Volharding* was just a few miles downstream at Old Windsor. Jolyon came up from Embercombe and joined me the next day, and together we gradually chugged the miles that separated us from our goal. When we finally saw her there was a sharp intake of breath and then silence.

Volharding is now berthed in Crinan on Scotland's west coast. She escorts people on voyages of self-discovery where they can question, probe, imagine and journey. When poetry, stories, music, and companionship join with the sea, wind, sky, sunlight and horizons, far-reaching changes are possible and happen. When the ship that carries the people is textured with a history of carrying real cargo, and is largely operated by pulling on ropes, winding winches, and heaving on a big wheel, then it becomes deeply uplifting. When the seascape is the western isles of Scotland, and the veil is so thin that you can almost walk straight through it, then anything is possible including the transformation of a life. Boats love leaders. They talk to us in the language of symbols, and so directly that you need the skin of a rhinoceros to miss it. We build our ship and provision it. We assemble the crew and assign roles. We study the charts, identifying hidden and obvious dangers, and we weigh anchor. At this point we have accepted risk – we are no longer in control. We have the weather forecast and we have the ship. Our skills, fortitude, experience, wisdom, everything that is part of us now bends to the task. Tides shift, squalls come and go, and our attitude to adversity, our self-knowledge, self-belief, self-honesty, all reveal themselves as the waves go higher. How often in life do we search the safe harbour, standing watch at night anxiously reading the buoys, our thoughts silently probing the darkness ahead of us. When we sail in this way we stand in front of the great dream that is life on Earth and we gain perspective. What happens from thereon is up to us, but we can never claim ignorance.

When an idea like this comes along, every now and then things move unbelievably fast. This was one of those times. I proselytised like a man possessed, deceived no one, and yet somehow it all came together. We bought *Volharding*. It is always best to buy a boat before you take account of what she will cost you to maintain and operate. To do otherwise brings only disappointment because even the most cursory speculation on costs will always reveal the same depressing fact – boats make no financial sense at all. They exist as something that creation has arranged to relieve the wealthy of excess cash and redistribute it. At this point Stephan Fritz happened along. Without his help we might have become broken on this particular anvil. It has cost a lot to restore *Volharding* to her current condition as a fully equipped, accredited, charter vessel – and it was worth every penny.

The sea is wild but it is not malevolent. The tsunami that took so many lives was not invested with hatred. I read several articles in which people questioned their faith on the back of the appalling devastation wrought by this disaster. 'Why did God let this happen?' It is so obviously flawed to invest either God or nature with the psychology of human beings. Earthquakes, floods, famines and plagues will always hover at our doorstep, but it is this same dynamic tension of creation and destruction that allowed life to flower in the first place. It was from the sea that we first emerged. Will we now curse her? Where nature and humans do meet, and where we are inextricably joined, is in our shared capacity for creation and destruction. The earth submits to no externally defined concept of perfection. It exists in the immensely challenging solar system, deriving energy from the sun while also ingeniously regulating its temperature – to our benefit. It is whole and in balance. This balance is not easily achieved. Huge forces of incalculable power are channelled, released, and held. Without any assistance from us, and a good deal of dangerous meddling, the Earth continues to give us the means to explore what it means to be human. Perhaps in her own non-human form the Earth herself grieves the death of her children. Far better than railing against the injustice of an earthquake would be to grasp hold of those things that do sit within our power to influence, and which now threaten worse disasters yet to come.

'In April of the year 1912 the *Titanic*, on her maiden voyage across the Atlantic, struck an iceberg and went down at sea. Long before the collision those in command had abundant evidence that icebergs lay ahead. The course had been set, however, and no one wished to alter its direction. Confidence in the survival capacities of the ship were unbounded. Already there were a multitude of concerns in carrying out the normal routine of a voyage. What happened to that 'unsinkable' ship is a kind of parable for us, since only in the most dire situations do we have the psychic energy needed to examine our way of acting on the scale that is now required. The daily concerns over the care of the ship and its passengers needed to be set aside for a more urgent concern, the well-being of the ship itself. Here is where macrophase concerns in one context become microphase concerns in another context. Passenger concerns in the situation of the *Titanic* needed to give way to the macrophase decision about the ship itself.' *

* Thomas Berry, *The Great Work,* Bell Tower: New York, 1999, p. 100.

CHAPTER EIGHT

Being and doing

A very positive outcome from my meeting with Niall Fitzgerald of Unilever was the arrival of an email that came out of the blue on the 6th January, 2003. Tex Gunning, Unilever Best Foods (UBF) chairman in Asia, had read my article 'Spirit in Business' after he had returned to the office from the New Year holiday, and he was moved to respond. He invited me to join him with more than 200 UBF Asian business leaders from seventeen different countries on a journey through the Guilin area of southern China. I emailed back immediately accepting his offer. I didn't know whether I was to be paid for this assignment, nor indeed what he expected of me in return, but I knew I needed to be there.

We gathered in Xingping village by the Li River. It was as if we had walked into another world. The land in this region of China is like no other I have ever seen. Stretching far into the distance is a landscape that seems born in the imagination of a painter. Limestone cones, reminiscent of termite hills, stretch into the distance, awesome in their magical faerie beauty. The vegetation is lush and verdant, and the river took my breath away. It is like standing very small in front of a storybook while someone turns the pages and invites you to enter. I had not met Tex until this moment. Visionary and intense, Tex is on a path unfamiliar to most business leaders.

We cannot force human beings in a sustainable manner to adjust themselves to the tyranny of conventional organisational logic. We can only let the organisation adjust itself to the universal needs of all human beings. We want to live meaningful lives. We want to live in service and care for others. We want the freedom and space to be creative. We want time-out to help, to grow, and we want to be part of an organisation that helps us to contribute to something that is far bigger than we could ever be on our own.

– Tex Gunning

On the way to dinner I asked him how he would like me to contribute.

'I'd like you to have conversations – about love, about spirit, about children, about trees. I'd like you to get close and help our people go deeper. Then, on the third night, I'd like you to tell them your story.'

That night I sat on the jetty wall, looking out across the deeply magical land that we would enter the next day. I looked at the village people still using technology that was familiar in Britain in medieval times, while at the same time having TVs and CD players. I looked at the UBF managers – the top UBF teams from almost all of the Asian countries – and I felt the hand of destiny on my shoulder. We may dream of work that is supremely fulfilling, work that somehow touches us to our full depth and brings a calmness and wonder that poets have called joy, but I don't think that many of us find it. I have fought hard, and I have never given up believing that such a place exists, or that I can locate it, but to know that all your dreams, one by one, are being answered is profoundly shocking.

The next morning we were ferried across the river and began the first day of walking. If you take a look at the photograph over the page and then for a moment allow yourself to hear the sounds, and smell the smells, and sense your feet treading the earth of China on trails that are literally thousands of years old … If you allow the mist to drift about you, and you visualise women and men of many different races, different ages, following a path that curves softly, a ribbon spread gracefully upon the land, the fishermen still using trained cormorants to catch fish, the children, the gentle sunlight. If you imagine …

I felt love in life, on the faces of the children … At the same time, I felt ashamed that I have let myself stagnate for such a long time, failing to reach out for what I long for. Why did I accept being ordinary in my life? Why didn't I live up to my beliefs and what I have in my heart? – UBF participant

We walked and we experienced. We felt things, and there were a million conversations. Like any other business, UBF Asia wants to be spectacularly successful, but the means of achieving this matters to them. How they get there is as important to them as the goal itself. This journey was not an isolated one-off event, it is part of their culture – one thread amongst many – ongoing and constant.

The River Li at Xing Ping

When I got up to speak on the third evening, we were deep inside our journey. A blazing fire sent sparks up into the night sky, flames leapt and danced and the whole community of people sat round, delighting in the night. Outside of our circle there were grandmothers, grandfathers, uncles, aunts, mothers, fathers, children and animals from several nearby villages. It was as if the world's more vulnerable and less protected had gathered to witness our intention and our action.

I had written myself some notes and as I rose to speak I realised that I couldn't read them. It was too dark. So I tossed them into the fire. I looked up at the stars and into the darkness, feeling the presence of the mountains, the people, the history, the future, and I spoke about what I love and the journey that I have taken to find that love. It was the Invisible Path that I spoke of, and as I looked at these people I knew that there is hope.

The next year we continued our journey in India, and this year we would have moved on somewhere else had it not been for the tsunami. These journeys are dialogue trails; they also contain experiences that have the potential to change lives. They seek to bring the exigencies of work and values together in a synthesis that will benefit all. They are idealistic in the best sense, yet they don't avoid confrontation. They invite self-appraisal, and they evoke the desire to unify doing with being, purpose with meaning, and receiving with giving. Working with Calcutta's very poorest and dispossessed, honouring the village people of Rajasthan who had given us their sweetest water, we encountered wisdom and kindness in bucket loads.

I was happy to see the joy in the faces of children who came over to the campsite. It made me realise that we have a huge responsibility to create a better future for these children. – UBF participant

I am not ashamed to say that at times tears came to my eyes, and I found myself knowing that anything, even everything, is possible. Like every other giant business, Unilever has an enormously long way to go if it wants to achieve integrity in its massive sprawling operation. We cannot sell products that harm the environment while talking up social responsibility, and we cannot, must not, allow the ravening hunger of shareholders to dictate to our values and moral instincts. So we start somewhere, anywhere, and then we hasten to take ground. We invite people – me, you – to take charge of our world, together, in community. We encourage ourselves to the understanding that everything is possible, and that the time is now. And the world will change. Even in our lifetime. It is a choice of destiny, and it is written in the vast sweeping mystery of the Milky Way, in the worlds which have already been and of which we know nothing, in the unfathomable future, in the Invisible Path, in the story of our unfolding.

> In business we always remind ourselves that there is only one constant and that is change. However, we should also remind ourselves that there is another constant and that is our need to love and belong. We have to integrate our need to be human as well as business beings at the same time.– UBF participant

There was no similar journey in 2005. The money, the resources, the people – all gathered behind the tsunami disaster relief effort. I received a short message from Tex: 'We are fine but in serious pain.' There is always the time when we are given the chance to test ourselves against the razor edge of terrible loss. There is no glamour, no options to 'sit this one out', no politeness, no cynical asides, no time ... No time. There is grief, and grinding effort, and the useless uncontrollable wish that it had not happened – and the impossibility of giving comfort to the inconsolable. Yet with this, and as the months move by, the UBF team will have collected images and experiences indelibly describing who they are. It is so for all of us.

Isle of Erraid Journal – 12

A big wind today blowing in from the north-east. Azul has come to join me for a while. We walk out towards a bay we haven't visited yet. She leaves soon and the cottage will feel empty without her warmth. We walk along the narrows that we have named Freya's Beach, making it our own. The wind is against our backs, nudging us, shoving us along. Past the Faerie oak grove we go, then south-east over the headland. Coming over the grass headland we gasp with delight at the spread of golden sands, the myriad islands, the surf pounding so many shores, and the wheeling and crying of the gulls. There is a wonderful gift that life makes to us as we walk towards her. Peeling away artifice, setting aside layer after layer, finding the authentic, we become both stronger and more sensitive, more vulnerable to beauty. I couldn't go back now, even if I tried. Both like and very unlike Macbeth, I am so steeped in beauty that were I to try and walk back to the shore the ocean muses would bar my way.

We walk hand in hand some of the way, playing with a miniature frisbee, and laughing a lot. Then to one of the shores, and we run towards the wide sea and the breaking waves. The wind is still on our backs, pushing us to the water's edge as the tide surges in. A big wind. The waves held back, their tops dashed behind them. The wind shoving against the incoming tide piling the water up until she becomes impatient and thunders in, and in, and in. Like the hand of a giantess the sea just keeps riding in over the sand. Running at full tilt, we barely keep ahead of her. Pausing occasionally, we glance behind, and there she still is, frothing, gurgling, skipping and snapping at our heels.

On the way back we came across the most delicate sand art created by the wind blowing against a tuft of dune grass. About three of the leaves had been bent over occasionally and their tips were just brushing the loose sand so that perfectly formed circles were traced around them. It was so exquisite and fine that we sat and watched for several minutes held enthralled by the brushstrokes and the play of wind, grass and sand.

It is love that inspires me to everything I consider worthwhile. It is love that calls us now to heed the writing on the wall and come alive. Love, and nothing else, will heal this planet. But it will not be the kind of insipid, lisping love that informs the weak-minded. It will be a fierce love, a love that gathers our thinking, our emotions, our spirit flame, and our determination to translate this love into tangible and pragmatic actions. I think we have to stand close to the flame and risk scorching. There is already much written on the critical importance of consciousness and the power of the invisible to effect change. I know this to be true, but I also know that no wheat grows unless someone gets out of bed and plants it, cares for it, harvests it, threshes it, winnows it, grinds it, bakes it, and then, probably exhausted, finally, gratefully, eats it. I think the redwood trees love Julia Butterfly Hill for taking peaceful, non-violent, direct action. Without her and others like her, we would have already lost the tiny fragment of these extraordinary trees that still remain. As it is, you and I can still walk these silvan groves and speak with the elders. Our privilege was bought by someone else's courage and action. By love.

Love inspires leadership. In fact, without it I don't think there is any authentic leadership. Why otherwise would we endure all the challenges and trials, the risks, the vulnerability, and the frequent knowledge that we have not achieved to the level of our vision? Stories abound of women and men who, clutching love to their breast, have risen to the calling of the time and taken leadership. I think it was love that inspired Florence Nightingale to become a leader and to fight for what she believed and knew to be true. Love is a big power that is given to us by the earth when we are birthed in the sacrament of water and take milk from our mother. It is the finding of love that will bring forth the leaders we need. It is with each one of us and we only need to let go of our fear and she will be known to us.

> 'When you want to build a ship, do not start collecting wood,
> cutting planks and distributing work, but awaken in the heart
> of people the longing for the great and endless Sea.'
> — Antoine de St Exupéry

We have ships to build, and fast. May love be the awakening power that calls us to leadership and makes us great.

> '[A] mood of universal destruction and renewal ... has set its mark on our
> age. This mood makes itself felt everywhere, politically, socially, and
> philosophically. We are living in what the Greeks called Kairos — the right

moment – for a 'metamorphosis of the gods', of the fundamental principles and symbols. This peculiarity of our time, which is certainly not of our conscious choosing, is the expression of the unconscious man within us who is changing. Coming generations will have to take account of this momentous transformation if humanity is not to destroy itself through the might of its own technology and science ... So much is at stake and so much depends on the psychological constitution of modern man ... Does the individual know that [she] he is the makeweight that tips the scales?'*

Do we know this? The evidence so far, suggests not.

A while ago I had a conversation with a woman who has held numerous top jobs in business, is articulate, energetic and successful at pretty much whatever she turns her attention to. She is also warm, caring and considerate. We met over a coffee in the West End of London and were talking over some of the more pressing issues confronting our world. Worried and concerned about a broad spectrum of environmental and social issues, she was well informed. Yet as we talked I became aware that this was the extent of it – concern and talk. Rising from the table, she said:

'Still, there you go ... I mean, what can we do ...?'

'A lot', I gulped, trying hard to swallow and speak.

'Oh well. That's life. Let's meet up again soon.'

And with that she swept off to the next meeting. I watched her as she made her way down the street. A force to be reckoned with, and yet somehow still disengaged.

What is it that brings us to a point of change? The kind of change when we no longer accept being spoon-fed lies and vacuous trivia, but root out the information we need and take action. 'What could I do anyway?' is never spoken by someone who intends action. There are countless things that we can do, if we take the time to inform ourselves, and if we are prepared to accept that doing more of one thing means less of something else. Feeling helpless gets us off the hook. People find the energy, find the resources, and find the inspiration, when they reach a point of choice and make a decision to live a life that is bigger than their own self-interest or that of their families. We may not be able to alter the circumstances of our birth, and we may have to carry the scars of battles lost or won throughout our lives, but almost all of us can transform our own lives, and the lives of others, if we choose to do so.

There is a park in North London that I used to visit, and along the footpath that leads into the wood is a cottage, somehow forgotten and passed by. Outside the gate the elderly owner used to write an inspiring message to all passers-by, which he

* Carl Jung, 'The Undiscovered Self', in *Collected Works of Carl Gustav Jung*, vol. 10, Princeton: Princeton University Press, 1970.

would change from time to time. Everybody walking by that cottage would read his messages. They were so honest, direct and loving, many people were very touched, and sometimes people would leave small tokens of their appreciation by the gate.

'Do the right thing. It will gratify some people and astonish the rest'. – Mark Twain

Isle of Erraid Journal – 13

Walking back home the light shifts and the island dances into a dream
world. Huge black clouds gather and bunch together, great torches of light
stream out from the setting sun bathing the distant Gleann an Teampull
on Iona with golden glowing light. I see blankets of rain like long draped
curtains washing across the distended arm of the Ross of Mull. Gasping I
look all around me marvelling at the contrasts, until, stunned into
stillness, I witness a vast arching rainbow of colours more intense and
vibrant than I have ever seen before. Light pours from between torn
fissures in the high banked clouds, and amongst it all the sea surges and
tugs, chasing the wind that moans and sings amongst its beloved isles.
One minute previously it was all quite different, beautiful of course, but
diffident, restrained and masked. Now energy ... as across the land the
magician calls out to the powers and the land answers. I find myself
speaking aloud to the wind and making public a secret wish. I have the
sense of being heard.

With many others I am convinced that we need dramatic change, fast. The exploitative economic model that drives all commercial and industrial activity is now so powerful, vigorous and polluting that it threatens the core life-systems of our planet. Corporations are the engines that most conspicuously and energetically pursue this path. In the past it seemed to me that I could find no better place to locate my efforts towards effecting change than with the leaders of these vast organisations. With my experience in developing teams and leaders from the corporate world over this last twenty years, I was well placed to give it a go.

I've changed my mind. Business doesn't lead, it follows. It manipulates the market, encouraging us to buy its products and devoting itself to the fabrication of consumers who believe they need what is being offered to them. It fosters and values dependency. Nevertheless, the moment we assert our will and successfully voice our discontent, business falls over itself to oblige, so nervous is it of weakening our addiction. The customer is indeed king. But more than this, I have seen that in the majority of cases most business leaders are so deeply mired in the flawed assumptions of their world that they do not have the vision to become advocates of change. They will endlessly crank the handle of a system that is destroying societies, devastating the natural world, and even harming themselves – and hard as it is to swallow – *we are no different*. When these same people return home in the evening they live amongst us and they shop at the same shops. 'They' are us. In fact there is no 'them and us'. It is like the vegetarian who still eats dairy food, wears leather shoes, uses products of all kinds that include animal derivatives. We are implicated whether we like it or not. We can pretend that the corporations are the enemy, but all of us are employed by, eat the food, derive our power, fuel our cars, furnish our houses, bedeck our bodies, and take our entertainment from these same organisations. We can deride our politicians but someone keeps voting them into power. We are the problem.

If we always set our convenience and comfort ahead of every other consideration and seek out the cheapest goods, even when we know that huge social and environmental penalties have been exacted for the privilege. If we eat meat which is the product of inhuman, even hideous, factory-farming methods. If we want it all but shy from paying for it. If we judge and never lift a mirror to see whose reflection gazes back at us. If we insist on forever pointing the finger and laying blame – then we will not find our way to the centre of the labyrinth. Corporations are inhuman – which is to say they are not human. They are human created, and we allow them to do inhuman things. We allow them. In fact they are not really so powerful, because they depend upon you and me to buy their products. Their products? Our products. There is no dividing line. For as long as you or I draw lines it makes it ever more difficult for people to cross them. Governments and corporations, armies, cities, in fact any organisation of any kind has the capacity to assume monstrous characteristics that should make us tremble. It is their inherent ability to mask their destructive urges behind anonymity and some semblance of legality that makes them so frightening. In our wondrous creativity we have generated a concept that is eating us alive – a legitimate, admired, seductive system that places the accumulation of material wealth before all else. If we do not take action to disable this monstrous creation, we will stand witness to an ugly denouement beyond imagining.

> I am only one; but still I am one. I cannot do everything, but
> still I can do something. I will not refuse to do the something
> I can do. – Helen Keller

Walking alongside others, trying and sometimes failing to walk the talk, tucking paradox inside my pocket, listing under the weight of inconsistency, I choose life. The young man who wanted an adventure – who yearned for a quest – he has it now in some measure. He's aged, and carries lines of experience etched in his face. He knows himself. He is amused by what he sees of himself. He loves the Invisible Path, the way of destiny, his soul's great journey.

I choose life.

There are people everywhere and from all walks of life who are stepping out of the shadows and voicing their concern. People we know are taking action in the most startling, creative, and courageous ways, whether big or small. Some of these people come from business, and many do not. All are leaders whether or not they see themselves as such. They are influencing others by their actions, and through their inspiration and passion. Around the world small and big initiatives are being born that are the responses of dedicated and visionary people informed about the deteriorating global crisis. Although the task that confronts us is formidable, there is hope, and we have everything to win. Every single time that a conversation takes place which inspires or encourages or emboldens, we secure a tiny victory. There was never a more exacting or thrilling time to be alive. There are many millions of people just one step from entering the garden and picking up a spade.

Completing the first draft of this book, I left Erraid and travelled back to Devon. On the way there I took a detour via the Indian embassy in London to get a visa, and ten days later I joined two different programmes seeking to bring senior business leaders to a new vision of inclusiveness. For some time I have pondered how to write of these things that I love. I have heard people of similar mind to me advocate not using 'the S word', Spirit, and I have rejected this idea. I also reject the idea that I should pretend a more distanced, academic approach in talking of our Earth. I can't. It's impossible, and I would feel that after all her care and love of me it would be nothing less than treachery. I have lost my way, foundered, tripped, twisted an ankle or two, and with more clumsiness than grace found my way home. I'm not about to pretend that it was the research project for my MSc. Embercombe is the little valley I call home. It is also home to millions of other creatures. Some people think I own it, which is insanely ridiculous if one only ponders that thought for a moment. This valley has been here for thousands upon thousands of years, and I'll consider myself fortunate if, a few decades after my death, gentle laughter ripples amongst the tree clan when they regale the young saplings with the comic antics of a human they once gardened.

Now as these words count themselves down to completion I shall walk out onto the land at Embercombe and visit favourite places. I shall build a fire and sit out under the stars and breathe a prayer that this book may touch hearts and call forth action. When the fire is made and the night has settled in, when the owls have come to join me, and when I feel the presence of night enfold me, I shall begin to feed the fire with pieces of wood, the bones of tree friends who have given-away. With each piece of wood I shall whisper this prayer and my words will be held by the rising smoke and the wind will take them to the storytellers and the songmakers, and I will be ready for sleep when the last of the wood is given and received by the fire.

Grandmother Creatress, Grandfather Creator, sacred powers of the four directions, Mother Earth, Father Earth,

With all my heart I thank you for this gift of life, and the privilege of learning from you. I have said farewell to the island and I have left my gifts.

Now in honour of you and all life, I place these thoughts with the wind, these emotions with the oceans, these dreams with the earth and these imaginings with the sun:

May the old people find the comfort of belonging, guard the gardens, and honour us with their prayers.

May the children be always cared for, and grow knowing that they are
loved by all creation.
May the young women and men find their visions and place their
great strength and energy with you.
May all who fight for you be mindful of spirit, and never give up until
the work is done – always finding the well of renewal when in need of
rest.
May our business and organisation leaders find the inspiration and
the courage to accept the baton of responsibility and do what needs
to be done.
May political leaders of wisdom, integrity, and action step forward and
be recognised by the people.
May balance be restored between women and men.
May all peoples know water, food, shelter, freedom, respect,
education, and love.
May all who know, question, and all who doubt, find strength.
May all our relations witness the love of their human sisters and
brothers.

Eyes closed, and my breath slows preparing for sleep. The twin worlds collide as my
waking mind yields to dreams eager for their time. A shift, a quickened moment,
and I am aware that the wind has changed quarter, now swinging in from the west
once more. In the darkness and freedom of the between-worlds I recall my last night
on Erraid. I am there once more, a visitor invisible. A fine mist of salt-laden rain
dampens the land, and the dark robe of night is lain across the isle as she rests. In
the deep abounding freedom of the resting rational mind I see myself rise, go out
into the darkness and look up to the stars. Unseen on this occasion, but real to me
as breath is real, the Invisible Path holds vigil in the darkness. An ally, a friend, a
sentinel. I do not need to know what lies ahead. I shall be informed in due course,
but I thank the spirit of all things that revealed the path at my feet and illuminated
my life with so much love and beauty.

I think of friends and the many I have yet to meet and recognise. I think of my
brothers and their families and all that has been shared, I think of chiefs who have
given me their friendship, care and teaching, I think of my mother and her unfailing
love and wisdom, I think of my father and the letter he wrote to me shortly before
he died which I received once he had gone and returned to essence.

And I know one thing.
We are not born to avoid dying by lying low and playing safe.
We are born to live.
We are born to leave the garden more beautiful than we found it.

KEEPING QUIET

Now we will count to twelve
and we will all keep still.

For once on the face of the Earth
let's not speak in any language,
let's stop for one second,
and not move our arms so much.

It would be an exotic moment
without rush, without engines,
we would all be together
in a sudden strangeness.

Fishermen in the cold sea
would not harm whales
and the man gathering salt
would look at his hurt hands.

Those who prepare green wars,
wars with gas, wars with fire,
victory with no survivors,
would put on clean clothes
and walk about with their
    brothers
in the shade, doing nothing.

What I want should not be
    confused
with total inactivity.
Life is what it is about;
I want no truck with death.

If we were not so single-minded
about keeping our lives moving;
and for once could do nothing,
perhaps a huge silence
might interrupt this sadness
of never understanding ourselves
and of threatening ourselves with
    death.

Perhaps the Earth can teach us
as when everything seems dead
and later proves to be alive.

Now I'll count up to twelve
and you keep quiet and I will go.

*Pablo Neruda**

---

* Pablo Neruda, *Extravagaria* (trans. Alastair Reid), Austin: University of Texas Press, 1993.
Quoted in *Resurgence* no. 233, Nov-Dec 2005.

BIBLIOGRAPHY

Berry, Thomas. *The Great Work*, New York: Bell Tower, 1999.

Deakin, Roger. *Waterlog*, London: Vintage, 2000.

Dirie, Waris. *Desert Children*, London: Virago Press, 2005.

Freedland, Jonathan. *Bring Home the Revolution*, London: Fourth Estate, 1999.

Gage, Matilda Joslyn. *Woman, Church and State*, Watertowne MA:
Persephone Press, 1980.

Harding, Stephan. *Animate Earth*, Devon: Green Books, 2006.

Hartmann, Thom. *The Last Hours of Ancient Sunlight*, London: Hodder & Stoughton, 1998.

Howard, Helen Addison. *War Chief Joseph*, Lincoln: University of Nebraska Press, 1964.

Jung, Carl. 'The Undiscovered Self', in *Collected Works of Carl Gustav Jung*, Volume 10,
Princeton: Princeton University Press, 1970.

Lorca, Federico Garcia. 'Yerma' and 'Blood Wedding', in *Collected Plays: Volume 1*, London:
Methuen, 1987.

McIntosh, Alastair. *Soil and Soul*, London: Aurum Press, 2002.

Neruda, Pablo. *Extravagaria* (translated by Alastair Reid), Austin: University of Texas Press,
1993.

Orr, David. *Earth in Mind*, Washington DC: Island Press, 2004.

Sachs, Albie. *The Soft Vengeance of a Freedom Fighter*, Cape Town: David Philip, 1990.

Tarnas, Richard. *The Passion of the Western Mind*, London: Pimlico 1991.

Watson, Julian. *Hoggie,* London: Hollis & Carter, 1949.

Wheatley, Margaret. *Leadership and the New Science*, San Francisco: Berrett-Koehler
Publishers, 1999.

Whyte, David. *The Heart Aroused*, New York: Currency Doubleday, 1994.

Whyte, David. *Crossing the Unknown Sea*, London: Penguin Books, 2002.

Williamson, Henry. *Tarka the Otter,* London: Puffin Books, 1971.

Williamson, Henry. *Salar the Salmon*, London: Faber & Faber, 1961.

Worldwatch Institute. *State of the World 2005*. New York: WW Norton, 2006.